Defining Your Boundaries

The YES | NO Playbook to what you want in life

Your Journey Guide

Introduction..05
Chapter 1: The Day the World Stopped...................15
Chapter 2: It's Your Choice...............................29
Chapter 3: What You Control..................... 37
Chapter 4: Setting Standards in Your Life............ 45
Chapter 5: What are Boundaries?.......................57
Chapter 6: What Shapes our Boundaries................71
Chapter 7: Why do we need Boundaries?...................83
Chapter 8: Material & Time Boundaries?....................99
Chapter 9: Physical & Sexual Boundaries?................107
Chapter 10: Intellectual & Emotional Boundaries......115
Chapter 11: Spiritual Boundaries.........................131
Chapter 12: Armed by Mental Boundaries..............145
Chapter 13: Understanding Your Basic Rights.........157
Chapter 14: In Tune with Your Feelings..................171
Chapter 15: Communication...............................181
Chapter 16: Pulling it Together...........................199
Chapter 17: Enforcing Boundaries......................213
Chapter 18: When Boundaries are off-kilter...........227
Chapter 19: Finding Your Happy Place..................235
Chapter 20: Breaking out of Panic Mode................247
Chapter 21: Giving up Your Boundaries 255
Chapter 22: Keys to Success...............................263
Chapter 23: It's in YOU!...................................275
Chapter 24: What's the Price You Pay?..................285
About the Author...291
Appendix...293

Introduction

"Jen, do you have a minute? Can you stop by HR?"

I smiled as I saw the message pop up on my laptop. I had just sat down at my desk after a meeting with my boss and peers, now HR was calling me in at the end of the day, I am pretty sure I know where this is going.

"Sure thing. Be right there."

I grabbed my wristlet, my phone, the necessities of what I'd need if I was walked out the door.

Hard not to be skeptical when you work for a company that has had so much instability and has gone through round-after-round of lay-offs. New leadership comes in, changes are usually bound to happen.

Our business in Asia Pacific was being impacted by some virus, and revenue for this distressed company was already lower than anticipated. Cuts were being made, and the higher you climb in a company, the more visible of a target you become when the going-gets-tough.

As I made my way to the HR department, I saw the face of the woman that had been deemed the 'terminator', since she was the one responsible for notifying employees when they'd been laid-off. I don't envy her job, that can't be an easy one.

"Jen, come this way."

And there he was, my boss, and then I knew. My premonition had been correct.

"We've made some changes, today is your last day, we wish you the best of luck."

And then he left.

That was the last I saw of my boss, we had 5 months of working together, and in 3 short seconds, we parted ways.

"Jen, here is your packet of information for your termination" "Sign on the bottom." "What do you need us to get from your desk?" "Do you have any questions?"

I had been with the company for almost 4 years; it was a good ride while it lasted. Wasn't my favorite job, wasn't my worst, I was pretty neutral about it, at best.

It's funny when these things happen, it's like turning someone's life upside down. One moment, you think you have a paycheck. One moment, you think you have health insurance. One moment, you have a 401K and paid time off. One moment, you're comfortable with where your next meal will come from, the payment for your home will be taken care of, you're able to provide for your household. Then, it all changes. My four years had been consolidated down to the size of an amazon package, I was given a packet of information to read and sign, and I went on my merry way.

Did I have any questions? Sure, I had plenty, but it didn't really matter at that point. My life wasn't going to change or be impacted if I had answers, I was just going to have to move on.

It's a phenomenon when these things happen, it's like there's a flurry of thoughts and emotions that not only happen to you, but to anyone else that was impacted by the change, or really anyone that knows you. My phone was immediately blowing up from friends, coworkers, vendors, anyone that had heard the news. There I was, with a box, riding in my Uber to go get my taxes done, and an inbox on my phone of texts that ran a mile long.

"Are you OK?"

"Are you going to be OK?"

"That was classless."

"I can't believe that just happened."

"I'm so sorry you're dealing with that!"

"I have so many emotions right now."

"Let me know what I can do to help."

The truth was, I was fine. It wasn't totally on my 'to-do list' for the day, but I had learned to accept what happens to me and move on. Sure, all those thoughts of food, shelter, health insurance all ran through my mind, but I also had this amazing overwhelming sense of freedom. If there was one thing I had learned from having gone through my own RESET™, it was the set of tools to help me get through these situations.

I think the people in my life were more distraught than I was, honestly. People had anger toward my company, they were disgusted how it all happened, they talked trash about the future of the company, and yet I was nonchalant about it.

"Gahhhh, you're too calm!"

Maybe, but what was I going to do, stomp my feet and go into a panic attack? Truthfully, the old Jen might have. I had learned to put up boundaries in my life, and *no one can steal my joy* was a standard I set in my life, so my boundaries went way up when this seemingly life-changing event happened in an instance.

Boundaries. It's an interesting concept, and I think of

them like the bumpers on a bowling lane. They keep us from going in the gutter, like I very easily could have done as my four years of 'stuff' got handed to me and I was told 'best of luck' and walked to the elevator. It's funny timing how life works, I wanted to write about boundaries in my next book, but I was struggling with finding the time where it would fit into my busy schedule. I was managing a full-time job and getting my business moving on the side. I was burning the candle from all ends. But, then I was gifted time, and here I am 15 hours after being laid off and I'm using the gift. I didn't think my intro would be about me getting laid off, but it's amazing how life will line up if you accept, pay attention, learn from lessons, meet the challenges and keep that positive spirit about you!

The most powerful chapter I wrote in "RESET" was on standards and boundaries. I was laying by the pool down in the Gaslamp District in San Diego, and I all too vividly remember my fingers pounding on the keyboard as I wrapped my head around what I had learned about boundaries and how I wanted to communicate that message. For hours my mind tossed around the concept, and dug deep into my soul. I took a hard look at what I had learned, and as I finished writing the chapter I had this feeling in the pit of my stomach: I had a lot more work to do in my own life, I had only scratched the surface on establishing boundaries.

I had this elevated sense of freedom and mastery as I

finished the chapter, I felt empowered by the words I had just written. I felt like I had just made it to another level in a video game, one that I kept failing at, but had now just received my golden star. I had elevated myself to a level of untouchable. I discovered that all I needed to do was put minor tweaks on my brain processes, and nothing could steal my joy. Nothing could take my happiness. Nothing could make me feel lesser than the person I believed I was. It was all about boundaries.

As I started digging myself out of all the barrage of texts I received, and I couldn't help but focus on this word 'boundary'. I not only dealt with the situation of being laid off, but then I had to weed through the thoughts, opinions, projected feelings of everyone that was so kind to reach out. No one was trying to bring me down, but I easily could have taken that path.

It was clear that everyone that was communicating with me was upset with the company and felt badly for me. They messaged me out of care and love, but I easily could have easily turned those comments around in my head to fuel anger in my soul.

How could they have done this to me? Don't they know I have a house and property I'm trying to sell, I have an apartment and bills, and now I have no income?! How classless is this rotten company! Garbage, I put in four years and got a box and a good luck. Screw you, company!

Honestly, none of those came to mind, because the bumpers in my mind kept me in my lane. I understood that people reaching out to me was nothing more than care and concern, and I was so grateful to be loved. I could choose to interpret their comments and internalize any negative connotation, or I could accept their care and concern and move on. The company letting me go was nothing more than a financial and business decision. The gift of time was a blessing.

I am untouchable, and those bumpers in my mind are what keep me on the straight and narrow. I feel impenetrable. When I put the standard in my life of me first and not letting anything steal my joy, getting laid off was certainly a test. It's like I could see the ball bouncing in between the lanes as different people, thoughts, and comments ricocheted in my mind.

THEM	ME	THEM
Your company is classless	I matter **I will win** I am valuable	How will you pay your bills?
What are you going to do?	**I am loved** I choose happy	Screw that company

Sure, I was getting close to the edge of the gutter, but my internal dialogue kept me moving toward the pins at the end of the lane.

It's time. It's time for me to breathe boundaries into life. I didn't know it when I woke up yesterday and went to work, but I knew it when I woke up today with the endless possibilities of what to do with my day that it was time.

I've had a few conversations with people recently and they told me about hardships they're going through: girlfriend broke up with them, got laid off, car smashed into them. All not easy things. I told each of them how excited I was for them, and they all scrambled in their brain as I shifted the dichotomy and dropped a positivity bomb in their stew of negativity. It's boundaries, it's perception, it's taking those challenges and allowing them to strengthen you.

I want you to become untouchable. When life happens, I want you to smile and say, 'what else you got'. I want your friends to look at you with two heads when you get excited for them when they're going through a trial. I want you to radiate happiness because it's the boundary you've put in your life and nothing steals your joy. I want everyone to want what you have.

Boundaries.

We're going to walk the steps to get you to that next

level, so you too can have that 'ah-ha' moment. Grab your bowling ball, and let's get ready to win!

Chapter 1: The Day the World Stopped

The world celebrated as the ball dropped, the lucky 2020 had arrived. Loved ones kissed under the mistletoe, men got down on their knees and proposed, the world celebrated the new decade as they enjoyed the luxuries of a booming economy. The United States had one of the strongest economies of its time, the stock market teetered at unprecedented highs. Well-deserved plans were made to celebrate the hard work everyone put in to make such a great nation. The US was historically known for long hours in the office and taking a fraction of the vacation time the rest of the world got to partake in, and a vacation or two was well deserved and earned in this upcoming 2020.

But the shine of a new decade, the optimism for wedding celebrations, the anticipation of graduations, the intense training for the Olympics, the planned family vacations all came to a screeching halt within a matter of weeks.

The world sat and watched as COVID-19 (Coronavirus) infected thousands in the unknown town of Wuhan, China. A disease most of the world was unfamiliar with, and one that would end up impacting all of the almost 8 billion inhabitants. We watched from afar as the disease began to spread, but it seemed too far to really hit home. Within a month, and no sooner than the promising 2020 began, the entire globe was forced to react, because this was big, and it was spreading with a vengeance.

Not even a week after I was laid off, the entire United States was told to go home and shelter-in-place. We watched as the economy took one of the biggest dips any of us had ever experienced, and we were on a roller-coaster full of fear and unanswered questions as we waited patiently in our homes.

Social media started blowing up with messages around panic and hysteria, people began going to the stores and stocking up on items. Shelves were completely wiped out, toilet paper was on backorder for weeks. Pasta, tuna, cheese, hydrogen peroxide, bleach, and hand sanitizer became the most sought-after items. There was a rumor that drinking bleach would kill this virus, a rumor that needed to quickly be debunked by professionals. It's amazing what people will do when they're driven by fear.

The virus began in China, but quickly we watched it spread around the globe. Italy and Spain were hit particularly hard, given the close proximity of the people in the towns and the elderly population. We all watched in disbelief as the numbers continued to rise from countries across the ocean, until it finally began to spread in the United States. From the comfort of our homes, we watched the number of deaths rise, and the number of impacted seemed to be growing daily by the thousands.

The virus infected millions of people globally. Astonishing to watch, unfathomable to comprehend, and an unimaginable amount of people affected to grasp. Race, gender, ethnicity, wealth, age: none of which had anything to do with spread of the disease. It was truly a virus that didn't discriminate nor hold back in the wrath of its impact.

It's easy to get caught in the panic when it's everywhere you turn. Restaurants and hair salons were closed down, bars were told to shut their doors, events were canceled, and President Trump even banned almost all international travel, no one in and no one out.

What a time to be alive. My world had gone from going into the office one day, to being laid-off, now forced to shelter-in-place with the rest of the world. Many, like me, were also left unemployed, many also probably left without health insurance.

Jobs were sparse, the reality of obtaining one or even getting a response from a company was bleak. Both of my properties that were for sale lost all interest from potential buyers, no one wanted to move, no investors wanted to invest. The entire world watched the pandemonium of investors start to pull out money from the stock market and many watched their life savings get cut in half. Those were the lucky ones, at least they had money to pull from.

There were many that lived paycheck-to-paycheck that were told to go home and wait.

Wait! How does the world wait?

Bills need to get paid, mouths need to get fed, and the world must go on. But how do you wait when the world is told 'you're laid-off', your industry no longer exists, and you just have to pause for some unforeseeable time this deadly virus to pass.

Families were now forced to be at home together 24-7. Children had to complete their schooling at home, while most parents were forced to oversee their child's development, a role many had never played in an academic sense. Everyone was trying to recreate structure and find a semblance of 'normality'. There were some families that had not come together in years and now were forced under one roof and told not to leave the house.

In a day and age where we can ask a device on our counter what is in the news without having to touch or type our inquiries, where social media consumes a large majority of people's lives, where we can have group chats on text messages, play games while chatting with our competitors located around the globe, the news, the impact, the reality was hard to miss.

From the high of January 1, to the social distancing and government mandate to stay at home two months later, the world watched and waited as we saw the death toll rising, not knowing when a cure or the end would be found.

I called my 88-year-old aunt on the phone and not even she had anything relatable from her lifetime. For the elderly population, and understandably so, it was a frightening time. Statistics proved the Coronavirus had greater mortality rates with the elderly and those with pre-existing conditions. She had asked if I wanted to come spend some time with her, and although I very much wanted to come see her, I also didn't want to be a vector of the disease. COVID-19 was an asymptomatic disease that could have been transferred without even knowing it. The grief I would have endured if I had transferred the disease to my beloved aunt would be more than my conscious was willing to take a chance on, so I respectfully declined her offer until after the crisis subsided.

Everywhere we looked, life was unrecognizably turned upside down. Albeit from fear precipitated by the news, the massive unemployment rates, the uncertainty we felt not just about ourselves but in sharing air with others, the fear of a hug or coming too close in proximity to someone, to washing our groceries, to watching time pass by as we sat on the ledge of the window. Life had changed overnight.

Protests started to breakout, political slandering and blaming ratcheted, the virus was not only alive in the world, but souls also were on fire.

Coronavirus. A disease that very few knew in January 2020, and a word that no one could avoid by February.

Not one of us that lived through the pandemic will forget what it was like or the impact it had. And if you didn't live through it, I would bet the gravity of the situation, that rock you feel on your chest that won't move as you try to inhale deeply, the sorrow you felt for everyone as they hunkered down has you in a solemn mood. To be honest, that's how it was for many, but not everyone.

There are two ways of looking at life, and there are always choices. Factually speaking, there were millions that were infected, thousands upon thousands that died, billions that were impacted, but it doesn't have to be all doom and gloom. There is an optimistic side, there is a other vantage point.

Boundaries.

Well, that's one way of looking at it.

Arm your mind and your life with boundaries and even in the most earth-shaking experiences you can see the silver-lining.

So, let's try this again.

Let's Try it again

The world celebrated as the ball dropped, the lucky 2020 had arrived. Loved ones kissed under the mistletoe, men got down on their knees and proposed, the world celebrated the new decade as they enjoyed the luxuries of a booming economy. The United States had one of the strongest economies of its time, the stock market teetered at unprecedented highs. Well-deserved plans were made to celebrate the hard work everyone put in to make such a great nation. The US was historically known for long hours in the office and taking a fraction of the vacation time the rest of the world got to partake in, and a vacation or two was well deserved and earned in this upcoming 2020.

No sooner did the decade begin, than the strong willed and tenacious leaders of the world were all brought together at one table with one topic to discuss: the Coronavirus. Unseen to the world, no one could have predicted the spread and the impact. As quickly as it was discovered it had already spread. Since it was an asymptomatic disease (where someone could be infected for up to two weeks without any symptoms), the spread was unknown to anyone. For the first time, the world watched the leaders rally together in their efforts to contain what proved to be a deadly disease. Regardless of political opinion, past relationships, or any other angst between countries, there was one thing they all wanted, to protect the people of the world from the spread of this virus.

None of us had seen anything like it. And although many had upcoming plans in 2020, we knew that this was something that needed to be taken seriously. This was a disease that didn't discriminate, and we would need to adapt to the new world order.

Although disappointing, the sweeping spread of the disease and the unfamiliarity with it justified the leaders decisions, even the highly anticipated Olympics were postponed, which again, would impact the majority of the world.

As I sat in my apartment feverishly working on projects and building my business out to a full-time endeavor, my old colleagues kept me informed about the mandates to work from home. Even though I had been laid-off, I was grateful the company was adapting quickly, and even more grateful the company had the infrastructure in place to accommodate a work from home scenario. My team's health and wellness were paramount, so I was grateful they could not only have a reprieve from the daily grind of the traffic, but were safe and sound in their homes.

None of us knew what to expect in the months to come. Like good girl scouts and boy scouts, America flocked to the grocery stores to buy survival packs, anything to get them through for an unknown amount of time. Pasta, tuna, cheese, water, hydrogen peroxide, toilet paper, bleach, and hand sanitizer flew off the shelves, all the foreseeable necessities to stay home for a duration of time. Parents loaded up on medicines, anything they could anticipate they might need to protect their loved ones during this time.

The response of the leaders was validated as we saw countries like Italy and Spain get hit especially hard. There was no denying the pandemic spread easily and certain demographics were at a higher risk for mortality. Although it was a shift in how we knew life, we had to keep the faith that our leaders were going to get us through.

There was an almost immediate response from the federal government in getting aid to the citizens that had been negatively impacted financially. Trillions of dollars were approved to support individuals, small business and money to re-stimulate the economy.

Banks offered to defer mortgages for a period of 90 days, evictions were banned, hotels were refunding non-refundable reservations, airlines were crediting and refunding tickets. The shift in the day-to-day routine happened over night and everyone was trying to adapt as quickly as they could. The United States Bartender Guild set up a National Charity Foundation for unemployed bartenders, companies were setting up GoFundMe accounts for their employees, celebrities like Mark Cuban (owner of the Dallas Mavericks basketball team) paid for salaries of those employees impacted by the layoff, one feel good story after another.

A pandemic that infected millions globally, brought 7+ billion inhabitants together on one mission: survival. Race, gender, ethnicity, wealth, age: none of which had anything to do with spread or the impact of the disease. It was truly a virus that didn't discriminate nor hold back in the wrath of its impact, nor did it have any limits on the kindness, generosity, and the renewed sense of spirit it gave us all.

It wasn't that some were affected while others were omitted, we all were affected. Granted, some were more impacted than others, but not one of us did not have a part to play. This was the first time the world was forced to all work together: as both nations and as mankind.

What a time to be alive. My world had gone from going into the office one day, to now laid off and forced to shelter-in-place with the rest of the world.

Now what? It's honestly not a question I asked myself.

Never once did I look negatively at the situation that presented itself to me. I had been gifted time, time that I so desperately needed. My list of to-do's and self-projects were piling up, and this was dedicated time to focus on getting them done. When do we have time to take a step back from our lives and take a breath? Sure, I didn't have my corporate job, but I had faith that my country, and even bigger than that, my God, was going to take care of me.

This was my time to go full in on my dreams, not just part-time. My life had become so busy, so frantic, I was grateful to have a breath.

No more 4:30am alarm clock, followed by a workout at an hour that most are still sleeping. No more long commutes, no more repetitive meetings with little progress, no more skipping lunch because I felt guilty leaving. No more getting home when it was dark out, no more working until my bedtime, only to wake up and do it again. No more working all throughout the weekend, allowing myself minimal downtime to relax. My life was entirely too busy, and I knew it was a matter of time until I shifted to making my business become my full-time focus where my passion truly laid. I don't miss those days, and in the exact moment I got laid off I felt this wave of peace and I exhaled with agreement.

Ever been on a roller coaster and you keep going up

and up and up until you reach the top, and you know your heart is about to get flung around? The climb to the top ends and you're launched into twists and turns, you're upside down, and your stomach launches into your throat. It's fun, it's exciting, it's palatable because you know it's temporary. You get to the end of the ride and you let out a sigh. You don't know if you just had fun or if you just wet your pants, but you are grateful you are still alive.

How many of us are riding through life on a roller coaster and it all too often feels like your stomach is just sitting in your throat? When was the last time you were given time? When you had time, did you use it? If you had time, what would you do with it?

The pandemic did just that, it gifted us time, all of us. We all had to take a step back from our grind and take a pause. Sure, we could:

- get wrapped up in the hysteria on social media, the alarming statistics we saw on TV, we could panic over the fact we were laid off.
- OR, we could take a deep breath and be grateful we were alive. We could use that time we had been gifted and work on a project, improve ourselves, spend time on the phone catching up with friends and family, and finally relax.

There are two ways of looking at every situation, and your mind controls both. I don't doubt that you felt some level of anxiety and fear as you read the first part of chapter. The two parts are identical, go back and read them, the only thing that changed was the perception. Your perception is your reality. If you entertain chaos, anxiety, if you feed into fear and entertain worry, then that is your reality. If you choose to look at the opportunity in the situation, if you choose to remain calm and find the good, if you look for the lessons instead of the hardship, then your world will be entirely different.

So how do you remain calm and stay positive when the world serves up an unexpected meal?

Simple, armor your mind.

You armor your mind to take you through life's journey so that when these situations arise you can walk through them with peace. Your boundaries are your bumpers on that bowling lane, those bumpers keep you safe. They keep you from going in gutter, and although you may bounce from side to side, you are still moving towards your target, and your target is happiness.

Coronavirus. A disease that very few knew in January 1, 2020, a word that was known by over 7 billion inhabitants by February, and an opportunity for the entire world to take a step back and assess their life as they knew it. It was an opportunity, for those that chose to see it that way.

Chapter 2: It's your Choice

The classic 'glass is half full' depiction. How many times have you heard that saying, and how many times have you thought about the power in those four little words?

Is it that the 'glass is half full' or rather that the 'glass is half empty'? Same cup, same amount of water, and both are true. You have been given the power to choose what is real, what is truth. What you see may not be what I see, and what I see may not be what you see, but both are right.

It's not like math class where there's only one answer. Your reality isn't as cut-and-dry as a mathematical equation, there isn't one answer and there isn't a correct answer. You have been given the freedom to choose.

You've been given $100 for food this week. Do you *ONLY* have $100, or do you have enough?

Your friend bought you a gift card for a massage. Were you given a gift that you'll never have time to use, or are you eager for when you get the opportunity to treat yourself?

You've been laid off. Are you worried about how

you're going to put food on the table, or are you grateful for the ability to apply for unemployment?

It's tax season and you owe. Are you mad that you have to pay, or are you grateful that you get to pay taxes because it means you made money (and not everyone can say that)?

The stock market drops. Do you panic and complain about your hard-earned life savings going away, or do you look at it as an investing opportunity to buy while things are on-sale?

There's a pandemic sweeping the globe.

- Do you panic, or do you look at it as an opportunity?
- Are you scared you're going to die, or are you grateful you're alive?
- Are you constantly worried about paying your bills, or do you have faith the system is going to help those in need and to stimulate the economy?
- Do you get upset because the gyms are closed, or do you take the opportunity to try some on-line options?
- Do you panic in front of the TV all day and paralyze yourself in fear with the news, or do you make a list of projects and hobbies you've been wanting to do and finally take advantage of the time to do so?

- Do you allow your business to collapse because it had a physical presence, or do you find an innovative way to bring your business on-line?
- Do you give up, or do you keep going?

Did you know you had a choice? You have any and all of those options available to you, it's up to you to decide. Having a choice is power, and if you want true power then you put your mind where you want it to be.

Negative thinking, for many, is a survival strategy. It's a way to place blame, it's a way to avoid, it's an excuse. We get into this victim role which allows us to avoid responsibility and ownership. It's a way many people use to seek attention, 'look at poor pitiful me and what happened to my life. Do you have sympathy for me?'.

As a motivational speaker, I've never once been called on to tell my heartfelt story and leave people thinking that I'm a victim. Sure, I was stuck battling addictions for years. I was physically beaten and would go into the office making excuses for the bruises on my face and my body. I hated who I was and was suicidal. Could you imagine if that was the end of my story and I thanked everyone for the time and left? That doesn't make for a motivational story, that's me looking for people's sympathy to say poor me.

Not even I say poor me, because that's a choice I have.

My scars and my past gave me wings, they made me into who I am today. I will not be a victim, I will be victorious. I have taken myself from my own hell, through my own transformation, and I have made myself into an author, a life coach, and founder of a company, an entrepreneur, a motivational speaker, all because of my past. I chose to not have my past define me, I chose not to be the victim, I chose strength and courage and I chose to take my past and allow it to make me a warrior.

Now that's a motivational speech, and that was the choice I made in my mind on how to look at my life.

Playing a victim is the absence of ownership. I was physically and mentally abused, in that regard I was this man's victim in a literal sense. But I will not feel sorry for myself and I will not tug on your heartstrings and make you feel sorry for me. I have chosen to learn from that experience, to help others through my story, and to view myself as Wonder Woman- not a victim.

If you're looking to make change in your life, then first-and-foremost you need to understand that you have a choice. Are you even aware that you are spewing negativity, playing a victim, and putting toxic energy and vibes into this world that are probably impacting the people in your life? Do you acknowledge and take responsibility for that? I didn't, at least I didn't know for a long time until I finally started to self-reflect and take ownership of myself and my mind.

I've met people that tell me they have to be anxious for the future, there's too much at risk not to. I politely scratch my head and disagree. I don't believe you need to constantly worry and stress about the future, I think you can accomplish the same while you remain calm and develop an action plan. I'll say it once, and I'll say it again, **stress and anxiety does not equal outcomes.**

Have you ever walked into a job interview stressed out and unloaded on the hiring manager? You told him you needed the job so badly because you needed the money. You then proceeded to let him know of all the 'things' in your life that you were juggling, and how you worry about the future of your children going to college (the oldest is 7, but you're deeply concerned if you'll be able to pay for their college). The hiring manager sits back and listens while you have a quasi-panic attack in front of him, then he thanks you for your time. Before you walk out of his office you say one last time "I really need this job, I'm really stressed about life and this would really help me out. Thank you for your time."

Do you think you got the job? You might be the most qualified candidate, but if you walk in carrying the weight of the world on your shoulders, if you're a ball of stress, if you're a constant worrywart, then it may be a little off-putting. The employer will need to determine if that energy is right for the office, and if he felt a heavy negative vibe, it's probably not helping your chances.

I had an employee once that worked for me that rode life on an emotional rollercoaster. I didn't know who would be walking in the door day to day, that is if this person even showed up. I remember telling HR that this person was "emotionally exhausting", because it tested my patience to deal with the instability day-in and day-out. There was always some panic, some worry, some life circumstance, and I had to keep my mind at a distance so I didn't hop on this crazy train. I even had to interject and make it known that some of the behaviors, some of the discussions, some of the responses were not benefitting the team. It was a decision this person chose to make when they came to the office, but I honestly don't think this person was aware it was actually a choice at all.

I don't think any of us wake up with the intention to ruin someone's mood, to drag down an office vibe, to negatively impact someone's life, and yet we do. We can directly impact our sphere, we have that choice to put out positivity or negativity, but so many of us forget that it's a choice we make because we are too busy playing defense, our mind is stuck in the gutter, or we are caught up playing a victim.

Life always presents options, yet you might not realize it. It's easy to get caught in a defensive mode. The problem with always playing defense is you aren't moving toward the end zone. You're stuck defending the other team while they try to score. This is when the coach needs to call a time-out, pull the players together, and assess options.

Self-reflecting and being cognizant of your mind and your thoughts are key. You are empowered to make that glass half full or half empty. You are empowered to look at the pandemic as an opportunity. You are empowered to take control of your mind and find the good in everything, no one can take that away from you.

Understanding you have a choice in the first place is a fundamental concept you need to understand to make positive changes in your life.

- It's your choice to be anxious
- It's your choice to worry
- It's your choice to be angry
- It's your choice to be negative
- It's your choice to panic
- It's your choice to hate
- It's your choice to stress
- It's your choice to be discontent

Wouldn't life seem a lot more appealing and optimistic if we could eliminate all of those feelings listed there? The truth is you can, and it's your decision if you choose to or not.

The power is in your mind, and connecting with it will

allow you to block those emotions, those feelings, those thoughts. First, you must understand it's a choice, it's your decision on how you view your world.

Once you grasp that concept, you start to build the foundation to armor your mind. All of those negative feelings and responses are found in the gutter of that bowling lane. All they are doing is leading you down to the end of the lane where you will get a whopping score of 0 because you will not have knocked down any of the pins. The boundaries you set in place, however, will keep you from going into the drudgery of the path that recycles your ball to its starting place.

Boundaries will protect you, they will armor your mind. But, if you do not acknowledge that you have a choice, if it's easier for you to play the victim and not take responsibility for your own life, then it's very likely you'll keep sliding down that perpetual state of negativity.

You choose, you decide.

Your mind is your most powerful asset. Make it work for you and understand that it's a choice you ultimately make.

Chapter 3: What you Control

"Good news, there's someone interested in your property!"

That was excellent news. It was a property that I no longer intended to build on, and financially I wanted liberty from. It had been on the market for half a year, and I had dropped the price significantly making it attractive for buyers. Finally, someone had a vision like I did and wanted to buy this land that I had done so much work on to clear-off and clean-up. Although my plans had changed, I wanted someone to come build their dream home just as I had imagined.

"That's great! Keep me posted!"

Not even 2 days later the reality of the spread of the Coronavirus hit the United States and we all watched the world start to react before our eyes. No one had gone through a global crisis at this scale, and panic started to sweep over the entire world. Safety products flew off the shelves, there were backorders and shortages of personal protective equipment (PPE) such as facemasks and hand sanitizers for months.

The necessities for survival were being stockpiled in people's homes, everyone was preparing the unknown. The fear of survival and the desire for added protection brought a spike in gun sales.

Then, on Monday, March 9, 2020 the stock market crash began. We watched it continue over the course of the next weeks, where it took another dip on March 12 and again on March 16th. Only the crash of 1914 and 1987 experienced more severe dips (1). Investors started changing their strategy and looking at more 'solid' investments other than the volatile stock market. Those that had their investments tied into stocks were limited on reinvesting as they watched their money take a nose dive.

"Jen, bad news. The investor pulled out, he said it was just too risky."

I wasn't the only one that received that kind of statement. The entire world stopped buying anything except toilet paper and guns, who was out buying land? The entire real estate business became deemed as non-essential and all the realtors were told to shelter-in-place. It was as if a pause button was put on the world and we were told to go home and hide.

Here I was, eager to sell a property so I could have financial freedom to invest more into my business, yet we were all mandated to go inside and not come out until this pandemic was under control.

None of us could have predicted what that would look

like or how long that would take. None of us had seen anything comparable. Sure, there was panic over Y2K (when programmers were concerned that there would be a crash when internal computer clocks changed from 1999 to 2000). Most people stock piled necessities in their house and hunkered down with their family to watch the ball drop. We held our breath as we counted down, and then....the world continued on as usual. The only thing different was the fact we all now had a year's worth of water in our basements.

Sure, the economy fluxuates, it has a pattern of going in and out of hardships. The stock market crashes, the stock market recovers. We go in and out of recessions, the world goes on sale, we all panic, then it recovers.

But the pandemic, this COVID-19, the Coronavirus-none of us knew what to expect.

I knew I had a choice I could make in the matter; I could choose to panic, or I could choose to remain calm.

I sat down one evening and I thought through what was out of my control and what I had control over.

First, what is control. Merriam Webster defines control as "exercising restraint or direct influence over, or to have power over" (2).

There's that word of power again.

What Merriam is saying is that what we have power over what we control. So what exactly did I control and not control in this situation?

I did not have control:

- over fear of the investors
- over the interest of the buyers
- the stock market
- real estate being a non-essential business during the time of a pandemic
- when the world was going to resume to business-as-usual

I did have control over:

- how I responded (calmly or with fear and panic)
- the price I listed the property for
- asking for help from friends or family
- contacting the bank to put payments on-hold for 90 days

This helped me to map out my options and where I needed to invest my time. I made the choice to remain calm, I dropped the price of the property, I talked to the bank about putting a hold on my payments, and I let my folks know I may ask for help if it got to that point.

Situation handled. There was nothing more I could do

about it, and I certainly wanted to keep my spirits high and remain positive. I made the choice to remain positive, even though the situation was not ideal, the world was responding with pandemonium, and no one knew what tomorrow would hold. I then looked at what I controlled, and I operated within that space. Simple enough roadmap.

Here was my lane, it was what I had control over. Everything that I didn't control, those were gutter items. There was nothing that I could do about them, there was nothing I could do to impact them, there was nothing I could do to change them, so why put energy there?

When we put energy into things we cannot control then we are setting ourselves up to experience anxiety and negativity. I often think about how I used to drive around on the roads. Although I liked the experience of driving my large truck, I hated being in traffic. Even worse, I hated bad drivers. These drivers would irritate me and I would get raging mad. I would scream obscenities, throw hand gestures, use my large truck to irritate them to 'teach them a lesson'.

Bad drivers are the worst. But, did my actions inadvertently make me one of them too?

Then I learned the concept of control.

I do not have control over how others drive. I do not

have the authority and control to teach others a lesson on how they should drive. I do not have control if there is an accident on the road. I do not have control if there is traffic. All of those things irritated me and got me so worked up, yet I couldn't control one of them.

I do have control over my reaction. When I learned to put my energy into the things I could control, then that boundary in my mind was able to block all those negative feelings.

It's amazing when you take a step back and see what is making you anxious, afraid, fearful, most of those items are entirely out of your control. What if the key to your happiness started in understanding that you not only have a choice to be happy, but it comes from understanding what you do and do not have control over?

It's so basic. You have a choice to be positive or negative. You have things in this world you control and that you don't control. Understanding the difference and focusing on what you do control will increase your likelihood of happiness. Of what you do have control over, you can choose to look at those things positively. These are all your choices! It's really quite as simple as that.

Let's look at the Coronavirus crisis:

- Do you control the death rate?

- Do you control the cure?
- Do you control the mandate to shelter-in-place?
- Do you control the government's response?
- Do you control the lay-offs?
- Do you control the stock market?
- Do you control the news station?

If you answered NO to those, then why would you worry about them?

How about the next list:

- Do you control your response?
- Do you control your happiness?
- Do you control how you keep yourself busy?
- Do you control who you communicate with?
- Do you control what you chose to eat?
- Do you control what books you read?
- Do you control the hobbies you like?
- Do you control if you turn on the news?
- Do you control how you structure your days?

Am going to guess that you could probably say YES to most of those. Although you may have some circumstances (children, spouse) or other commitments, you actually control the things on this list. This is where you need to focus your attention.

When you are focused on what you cannot control, then you are a candidate for fear, panic, worry. I'm not suggesting you turn a blind eye to the world and not educate and inform yourself of what is happening. What I'm suggesting, however, is you not put your energy and efforts into what you cannot control, but instead put that time and attention into what you do.

How do you navigate the world and keep out that negativity? Sure, there's the choice and understanding what you control, but what is blocking the negativity from keeping in? How do you armor your mind to defend you and keep you positive, in any situation?

Boundaries. Boundaries are your answer.

Chapter 4: Setting Standards in Your Life

Before diving into boundaries you need to understand standards. Standards are a level of quality you set for your life.

Ever thought about whether you have high standards or low standards? Think about your job, your companion, your choice of friends, your ideal date night, where you vacation, what activities your get your children into, the school you want your children to go to, the food you eat. I think most of us would like to think we have high standards.

Imagine going on a date with someone for the first time and you ask some general questions.

> **Q**: What's your ideal place for a dinner date?
> **A**: I don't really care, I eat everything. I spend most of my time in fast-food drive-thrus, so I'm ok with a cheap burger from some place fast and easy.

> **Q**: Must be interesting raising twin 13-year-old girls! What kind of curfew do your kids have?
> **A**: I let them stay out however late they want. They don't need to call, I trust they make smart decisions. If they really need

something, they'll call.

Q: Do you have any interests/hobbies?
    A: No, I like to watch reality TV, that's about it. Hobbies just take up my time.

Q: What's your idea of a perfect vacation?
    A: Someplace where I can go play video games and stay inside all day. I like to drink until I pass out, so there would need to be a lot of booze.

Q: What are your goals in life?
    A: To get out of bed and try not to spend all my money. I come from money, so I don't need to have goals.

Would you say this person has high standards or low standards? Probably low. I would be 1000% lying if I didn't tell you that last question literally happened on one of the dates I was on with a guy who apparently came from money. And my response was to not see this guy again because we clearly had two different ideas on the standards we should have in our life. I don't care how much money you make or not, I value having goals and objectives in life, so this was not a fit for what my belief system looked like. High standards does not mean a high bankroll, it's the beliefs and values that govern your life.

We typically associate ourselves with people that have

standards that are alike, these commonalities attract us to one another. Not all friends or people in your circle, or even your significant other, will have 100% the same standards as you, but very likely they will be in the same ballpark.

Ever met someone that chose to be a vegan because they didn't want to put things into their body that contained unnatural substances and yet they smoked cigarettes? Last time I checked, smoking is full of additives, which to me is about the same as putting food that has additives in your body. There are people, however, that place different standards on what their food intake should look like versus whether they choose to smoke or not. Standards are defined by the individual, and not everyone that sees them may agree with the rationale. By the same token, not everyone may want to date a vegan or a smoker, and that's their right to decide. These are standards that we place in our lives and they are our belief system that help us make our decisions, and clearly they can vary.

Standards are the beliefs that govern our life. If we are aware of it, or not, if you are old enough to talk, then you have a set of beliefs. It's our families, it's our upbringing, it's our social class, it's lessons, it's life that helps shape our beliefs. A child may not know that touching a hot stove will burn them, but the first time they do it- they'll never do it again. They have become a believer that a hot stove will bring pain, and it shapes their decisions and behaviors going forward.

If you have high standards in your life, then you believe that things matter. If you didn't, then you'd have low standards. That date of yours didn't care about what food was eaten, didn't matter if it was processed hamburger meat or low-grade hotdogs, it didn't matter. This isn't the same as you being open to a variety of different foods (sushi, Thai, vegan, Italian), you can still have standards within your choices. You have low standards if you don't care at all in regard to the quality, the preparation, the nutrients, and the experience, not the fact that you're open to a variety of options. Your date also didn't care about the objectives of a vacation, the main goal was to play video games and drink. It didn't include fresh air, exercise, socializing- all things that possibly you look for in your life.

You don't typically hear someone say, I prefer my spouse to have no standards. Could you imagine if you had someone that didn't care if their clothing was appropriate for different situations, if they slept around with other people, if they had zero regard for spending money and racked up massive credit card bills? What if that person decided they didn't like to put their dishes in the sink and just left them where they ate, and taking anything to the trash was out of the question? Spills happened and were never touched, the carpet was never vacuumed, clothes were never washed, and the toilet was never cleaned. Does the thought of that make you cringe? Why? Because you have a higher standard of cleanliness and hygiene that you prefer to have in your life.

Usually, high standards are good to have. You know that without doing certain things at a certain level that you are not going to get to where you want to go or ultimately be the person you wanted to be. For anyone that knows my story, I was so frustrated with myself because I was held captive to an addiction for decades, and it was a life I loathed because it wasn't the standard I identified with for my life. I wanted to be free from addiction and everything that went along with that life. It was holding me back from getting where I wanted to be and being the person I knew I was destined to be.

Standards are healthy and necessary for us to have in our life if we have a quality of life or objectives we are trying to achieve. They are goals, as small or as large as they seem, they are targets we set for ourselves. We set out to have good hygiene, we set out to have a good and faithful partner, we set out to abide by the law, we set out to retire, and we set out to be happy. These are all standards we set in our lives and we build our life and day-to-day based on these objectives.

Although high standards are good to have, if they are unrealistic, hurtful or unattainable then you may be setting yourself up for failure or missed opportunities. Imagine if you set out to find the ideal mate and it included: self-made millionaire, owned a business, perfect head of hair, no grays, physically fit and had a 6-pack, independent, funny, puts the lid of the toilet down after use, cooks, cleans, straight and white teeth, runs marathons, works out in the morning, Christian, tithes to the church, no tattoos, never been married, no kids, travels, values family and friends, never gets angry, adventurous...to name a few. Sure, this sounds like a nice list, maybe, but is it realistic? If you never find this person then are you missing out on finding love in your life? If your standards are unrealistic then they could keep you from experiencing joy, happiness, and could even hurt people along the way. Remaining cognizant of the standards you set in place will help you reassess if you need to make adjustments along the way.

Setting standards and knowing the direction you want to head is the first step in knowing what boundaries you want to put in place. These are the edge pieces of the jigsaw puzzle, the framework, and the boundaries are all the inside pieces you interweave to build your masterpiece. Establishing these will help you set up the right boundaries for you to achieve your goals.

Standards can be both acceptable and unacceptable

Unacceptable:
- Violence
- Abusive behavior
- Harassment

- Bullying
- Emotional abuse
- Discrimination
- Lying
- Promiscuity

Acceptable:
- Tell the truth
- Be respectful
- Be kind
- Abide by the laws
- Pay bills
- Faithful to your partner

Although these standards may seem obvious, there are many that could vary greatly depending on upbringing, surroundings, location:

Cultural:
- What age to start drinking coffee
- Tipping
- Standing in line
- Nudity
- Cursing
- Arriving on-time
- Calling an adult Ms./Mr. or Sir/Ma'am
- Asking someone their age
- How long you live with your parents before you move out
- Saying please and thank you

Standards may also be feelings or attitudes:
- Happy
- Anxious
- Angry
- Paranoid
- Fearful
- Positive
- Negative

Once you've set a standard in your life then your life has a goal, an aim, a target.

Using the bowling lane analogy, standards are the pins at the end of the lane, you are the ball, and as you know, the bumpers on the gutters are your boundaries. The goal is to get you to your target and to do so without going in the gutter. If you don't have a goal set, then you're just bouncing around aimlessly. To live a purpose driven life you need to establish goals and guidelines for yourself.

When you set standards in your life and make them a requirement, then you are committing to a journey. If happiness is your standard, then in everything you do you are committed to seeking happiness. If you want to avoid pessimism then you are always looking at that glass half full. Knowing where you want to be is going to help gauge your direction, response and actions along the way.

As life happens, it's likely you'll want to tweak and modify the standards to fit where you're at in life.

You might have set a standard in your life that you need to **have a job**. Good standard to have. Let's walk through what that might look like as you progress through your life:

Age	Goal
16	Get any part-time job that pays $8/hr. or higher to pay for movies, video games, concerts and gas
22	Get a job that requires the use of your college degree and gives you enough money to move out of your parent's house
30	Find a job that aligns with your career path with upward mobility. Make enough to live on your own and save money to buy a house
40	Get a job that supports a family, is stable, doesn't require you to move, management only, has great health benefits and a 401K
63	Find a non-stressful and enjoyable job to cover the bills as an individual contributor that has a steady income and has flexibility

	to work from home
68	Have found jobs throughout your life so that you don't have to be working unless you really enjoy what you are doing

As this person aged, even though the job was the priority, the standard of the job changed. At each age the standard continued to rise. Albeit the desire to just have any extra cash, the ability to move out of mom and dad's house, the desire have your own home, to live alone, the need to support a family, or finding a job that has no stress and allows you to work from home, or to not have to do a job unless you enjoy it, the goal was adjusted along the way to fit where in life the person was.

Raising the standard of having 'a job' doesn't always mean more money or a higher title, sometimes it may mean more happiness. When this person turned 63 they assessed the need to have more flexibility over their schedule and wanting the ability to work from home. Whereas before it was important to climb the corporate ladder and build their job title, when they got close to retirement age the simple fact of getting a paycheck and enjoying what you do was more important. Freedom, flexibility, reduced stress can all be examples of raising the bar in our life, and that too could happen at any age.

There is no right or wrong way to set standards in your life (as long as you are not detrimental to your health or others). You get to define your goals, your targets, your life objectives, and they'll vary as you go throughout your life depending on what variables you're working with.

Had this person continued to keep 'any part-time job' as the standard throughout his/her professional career, then it may have been impossible to accomplish some of the other objectives in his/her life.

Set your eyes on where you're going, and when you do, you'll have more purpose and direction for your life. To get there, you'll use boundaries, those will help you stay on track for your target. As we dig deeper later in this book and get past the fundamental definitions of standards and boundaries we'll address how they overlap. Let's dig in and take a closer look into boundaries and get a better understanding of what they are and why we need them, since we've established they hold the power to unlock our happiness.

Chapter 5: What are Boundaries?

Boundaries are the guidelines, the limits, that keep us in our lane and aligned with our standards. They establish how we should be treated. They tell us when and when not to do something. When we're moving towards our goals and targets, boundaries serve as the bumpers that keep us in our lane and keep us from landing in the gutter.

Boundaries are both physical and emotional limits that you put in place that should not be crossed. When they are, you may feel sad, anxious, depressed, angry, disappointed. This is why not only do we need to set them, but we need to enforce them, but we'll get there in an upcoming chapter.

Have you ever set a goal for yourself that you were going to start getting more sleep? Maybe this was something you had neglected in your life for a long time, and finally, you just found yourself not having the energy you needed to get you through the day. You read a study on sleep and saw it reduces stress, improves energy, helps aid in weight loss, and reduces inflammation- all issues you were dealing with in your life. Because your ultimate goal is to have a happy and healthy life, you decided that more sleep was necessary. With so much happening in your life and with work, it was really going to take some big changes, but you were committed.

At first, you started getting 6.5 hours of sleep. Not quite the recommended amount, but certainly better than 3-4 hours. You cut out TV, you asked your family to eat dinner earlier, you even agreed to fewer happy hours and work dinners. You were starting to feel pretty good about yourself. Your family was on board, and they were even benefitting from your extra energy. You seemed to be in a better mood all around.

Then, you were given a new account at work. You started working longer hours, and since you were going to get a big bonus if you could keep the customer happy, you said yes to everything. This required more happy hours after work, more work dinners, and before you knew it you were back to 3-4 hours of sleep a night.

You were irritable, you were tired, your waistline was growing, you kept having to tell your family you couldn't be present, and you were back to zero energy.

What happened?

You had a target, you knew your boundary, but you didn't enforce it.

When you were holding yourself to a goal, when you

were working towards a better quality of life, you used that to determine your path. You said no to happy hours because that would cut into your evening time. You didn't have to cut them out entirely, but 4 out of the 5 days of the work week you were committed to going home after the office. You modified the hour you ate dinner, you made the decision to turn the TV off at a certain hour. You made decisions in your life based off the goal to get more sleep- those are boundaries. Sleep was the goal at the end of the bowling lane, and anything that prevented you from getting there was the gutter. You established structure in your life (put up bumpers) to ensure that you were meeting your goals.

Easy to blame the new account on not getting sleep, right? Wrong.

You take ownership for your life, and this is nothing more than an excuse. If you have a standard or a goal that is important in your life then you'll make it happen. Does it present more of a challenge? Sure, but it's all still attainable. You didn't enforce the boundaries so they didn't happen. Can you still get that bonus for schmoozing the client? Absolutely. You don't need to stay until the end of happy hour, they just want you to pick up the bill. Stay for an hour then head home. Before you leave, either tab out or keep an open tab with your credit card on file. Either way, you've fulfilled your obligation to the new account and to yourself. You are leading the ship, guide it where it needs to go.

Those are boundaries. They protect you and keep you moving in the direction you want to be heading. When you or someone else crosses them then this could compromise your end state goal.

Boundaries can be both physical and emotional.

Physical boundaries include space. This lets people know how close they can get. Physical boundaries may vary depending on the relationship of the person. It might be ok for your spouse to put a hand on your leg during a movie, but it would not be ok for a random stranger. An emotional boundary may be if someone treats you as second class. You know you value yourself, so if someone else does not then they've crossed an emotional boundary.

Boundaries are sometimes rigid and sometimes they are loose.

You may have told yourself that you are committed to getting those 6.5 hours of sleep a night, and you could either go to bed early or sleep a little later. You give yourself a little flexibility on your nightly and morning routines based on priority. If there's a work event that requires you to get home a little late then you'll skip your morning workout to get the extra sleep. But, you've told yourself that you'll try to limit those late nights, so when your friends ask if you want to see a movie after work you decline because you know that both sleep AND the morning workout are good for your health. Although you enjoy movies, you know it can wait until with weekend, so you decline. You've given yourself some flexibility within achieving your goal, and they need to be assessed in the holistic picture of your life and your schedule.

Boundaries block out unwanted feelings (fear, panic, anxiety)

Boundaries not only keep you in your happy place, but they can block out what is unwanted. If you've set the standard in your life that you want peace and happiness then anything that doesn't align with those goals and standards needs to be reframed or eliminated. We'll dig into this further in an upcoming chapter, but know that boundaries protect the mind from what you don't want in your life.

Boundaries help give you identity and define you.

When you buy a house you get a survey of the land that goes along with it. This will help you as the homeowner know where you mow your lawn, where you plant your garden, which trees to keep manicured, determine responsibility if there's a storm and a tree falls over, etc. Those boundaries define your property and what is your responsibility.

Same holds true for the boundaries you establish in your life, they give you identity.

Let's look at Howard Stern, who is well known for his radio and television shows where he has makes off-color jokes and his topics can be rather direct and even crass. Not everyone loves Howard, but we all know what to expect. Howard has made an identity for himself that has captivated millions. He's known for criticizing or even humiliating his guests, and anyone who goes on the show has to be prepared for a direct, frank conversation with Howard.

Your boundaries will give you that identity and people know what to expect.

President Trump is another one with a very distinct identity. He has no issues with speaking his mind and the world has come to expect that he will tweet his opinions on matters. While some people are more reserved, Donald Trump is known for being very direct and to the point and is a key part of how we identify him.

Boundaries give you power over your life.

Boundaries give you control over your life. Control is power. You call your shots, and you let others know to respect you and your space.

Think of the legal system. There are rules and laws that are set in place. When someone disregards those rules then there are usually ramifications to their actions. The authorities have the right to prosecute, arrest, issue a ticket, etc. depending on the law that was broken. This is power the governing law has given them (with rules restricted around their practices as well).

The laws and rules are made to drive behaviors, and when they are not then consequences can be enforced. It's power.

It's the same power you have over your own life (let me be clear you do not have the same authority as the police to enforce penalties on other people). Establishing rules and laying down your own law is the same power, you decide. Although you do not enforce the law like the Police, you can decide if you need to have a discussion with someone to talk about respect and boundaries, or you may decide you need to remove someone from your space altogether. This is power, it's the power you own.

Boundaries improve your self-esteem.

When you have set a standard of behavior for yourself and you hold yourself and others to it then your self-esteem will improve.

Ever been in a situation where you walked away and felt badly about yourself? Maybe you told yourself that you were going to remain faithful to your companion, yet you found yourself flirting with someone and even liked it. Maybe you even took it a step further and it was a step you knew would be detrimental and hard to recover from with your significant other. You didn't think about it in the moment, but you really felt low about yourself afterward. It wasn't a behavior you imagined you would engage in, it was completely out of character for you. There was no way you could tell anyone, it was going to have to be your little secret, and it was a secret that was going to eat you up inside.

Maybe it wasn't the exact situation, but have you ever done something that didn't align with your character? Didn't make you feel good, did it? That was your self-esteem that was compromised.

Boundaries enhance your self-esteem because you know if you operate within them then you are holding true to yourself. If you have a certain standard or quality you have set for yourself and you stay within your boundaries then you are much more likely to have self-love and internal respect.

When you have both self-love and respect for yourself then your esteem will be higher and you will value your self-worth.

Let's flip that situation around. Imagine you are in the bar with some coworkers and a gorgeous human being approaches you and starts flirting by commenting on your outfit. Although you find this person attractive, it's clear the intentions would lead you down a path that would go against your moral compass and the boundaries you set out for yourself. You have promised to remain faithful to your spouse and this looks like a slippery slope.

"Thanks, appreciate the compliment, but I'm married and I'm here with my coworkers. Enjoy your evening."

Think how much better you would feel about yourself because you stayed true to you, your beliefs, and your spouse? You had two choices; to engage or to shut down the conversation. Engaging made you feel badly and lose self-respect, whereas asking the person to leave made you feel good that you did the right thing and ultimately gave you higher self-respect.

What about that time you turned down a job change at work because it was a lateral move that you felt did not give you the job advancement you were aiming for? Maybe it wasn't easy to look at your boss in the face and decline the job (it may have even cost you your job), but you knew that had you taken it that you would be living out someone else's idea of what your career path and potential would look like, not your own.

I've been there, and it took many years to get to this point. I bounced from job to job as my employer saw fit. The problem was that I was not owning my career path. I allowed it to be dictated by whatever boss I had at the time and whatever role needed to be filled. I kept wondering how I would get into these positions, and the reality was it was my lack of boundaries that allowed it to happen. I didn't feel good about the job changes, in fact, I even despised some of the positions I was directed to have. Not only had I given up my power, but I also didn't feel good about the direction my career was going. It wasn't so much that my boundaries had been crossed, I never established any, and it was game changing when I did.

I remember the feeling when I told my CIO that I was not interested in taking the job he had in mind for me. I remember how it felt to own that power and how good I felt about me standing up for my career and my direction.

Just because you have boundaries in place doesn't always mean decisions will be easy or that life won't change in unanticipated ways because of those decisions. It would have been much easier to go along with my boss' vision since he knew what organizational changes he wanted to make in the future. I spelled out where I saw myself, my end-state career goals, and what I felt would make me more well-rounded to achieve my career goals and objectives. In the end, my vision didn't align with any roles my boss had in mind, my current position had been eliminated and I was laid-off. Sure, maybe I would still have a job if I was willing to take the role that had zero upward mobility or use any skill sets I was interested in using, but I stood up for my career path. My boundaries were intact. I can always find another job, but I can't get back time. If I wanted to be serious about my career path then I needed to be affirmative in my direction.

It's not always the easiest path to take when you stand up for yourself. In fact, you may find that it takes you down a bumpier road or that people may not like you. But, when you stay true to yourself, when you are willing to hold yourself to a certain standard and don't allow anything to penetrate that, then ultimately what you'll find is a heightened self-esteem. I stayed true to me, my goals, my objectives, my career path, and I felt good about it.

Boundaries define how people can treat you.

Remember when your Dad would ground you and send you to your room for disrespecting your Mom? That was never a good moment. No friends, no tv, no fun, just sitting in your room thinking about your actions. Dad even took away the ability to communicate with anyone, he wanted to make sure this punishment was memorable enough so you wouldn't forget that it was not ok to disrespect the woman that brought you into the world. Now you knew, disrespecting Momma meant sitting in solitude. Noted.

Dad had a boundary with the way his wife would be treated, and crossing that would lead to repercussions. You knew very clearly what acceptable behavior was and what was not acceptable.

Let's say you run a business and one of your core values is honesty. Your employees know that dishonest behavior is not tolerated and could lead to being placed on a performance improvement plan or result in being let go. This includes lying, stealing or not being forthcoming about something that happened. The standard is honesty and the boundaries include anything that would not be considered honest. Those boundaries define how your employees will act in the workplace, how they treat you, and how they treat one another.

Imagine if you had no boundaries at work. People could come in and dress however they wanted, they could use any language they wanted, they could come at any time, they could leave when they wanted, and could even take lunch breaks for as long as they wanted. This could be a slippery slope into having a free-for-all at your company. Think about it, we all come from different backgrounds and have different ideas of how our lives should be governed. In the workplace or in your personal life you need to set the boundaries so there is a level of harmony that you can achieve, otherwise you deal with whatever someone decides is right, which might not necessarily be what you think is right. Boundaries will define how people should treat you or the situation.

~~~~

Boundaries are power. They help give you identity, they teach people how to treat you, they give you respect, self-esteem, they keep you operating in a certain happiness level and keep out what doesn't serve you, they govern your life. They keep out what isn't welcome and keep you operating in the space that keeps you moving towards your set standards and goals.

Establishing them is like those bumpers on the bowling lane. Those boundaries are protecting you, they're cushioning you when you get close to the edge. When you're about to cross them- they bump you back in the game, and they keep out what doesn't belong.

Chapter 6: What Shapes our Boundaries?

Much like standards, boundaries can have many influences that shape how we define and govern our lives. Two women, born on the same day from two different sets of parents, two different religions, two different sides of the world could have two very different sets of boundaries even have the same standards or goals in their life.

Let's look at Sarah in the US. Sarah was born to a secular family in downtown Chicago. Sarah's parents were on-and-off, sometimes they were together and other times they were off seeing other people. Both of her parents were heavy into drugs, though her mother did have some moments of sobriety and Sarah cherished those moments. She felt like she, in many ways, was the adult in the house: keeping it clean, getting food and cooking dinner, and even figuring out how to pay the bills sometimes. Sarah's upbringing was hard and was much different than a lot of her friend's upbringing. She remembers only once when she was given a real birthday gift, the other times she usually was given a $5 bill to go get a meal at McDonalds.

While most of Sarah's friends were growing up and learning to date, she found that she was learning to play men for their money- it was the only way she could survive. When her friends got their second ear piercing she already had a small heart tattoo on her shoulder.

Sarah was good about forging her mother's signature, which she had to do often because she would find herself sleeping past her alarm and needing to write a note excusing herself for being late. Everyone knew Sarah's situation was tough, and no one really believed the notes were from her parents. It was an issue, but Sarah genuinely tried to show up for school and get her coursework done (even if someone else was doing it for her).

She was doing the best she could with the resources she had and the cards she was dealt. When she was 16, she moved to California, far away from that mess, and graduation wasn't on her list of to-dos anyhow. She left a note for her parents and wished them the best. She cared, and she didn't, she was just tired of playing the role of the parent. Sarah wanted happiness and she knew it wasn't going to happen under her parent's roof.

Sruthi was born to a Hindi family in Bangalore, India. Her parents found each other when they were in college and fell in love. While many families still practiced the traditional arranged marriage, Sruthi's parents had a 'love marriage'. They did everything together, and their love for each other was infectious.

Everyone around them fed off their glow and their energy they had for each other. They were not only well grounded in themselves, but they made sure to have a close family unit.

Sruthi was good at school, her parents always encouraged her to follow her dream and they supported whatever she chose. She was excellent at music and on her 9th birthday her family bought her a baby grand piano. Sruthi would exercise her fingers across the ivories for hours, and the more she played the more her parents felt like they were at a concert. They were so proud of their daughter. She was their first born, their only daughter, and she was the apple of their eye.

Sruthi excelled in school and was given a full-ride scholarship to her first-choice college, her parents celebrated by throwing her a graduation party of her choice. She chose to have 30 of her classmates join her at Torq03 Sports for a night of bowling and go-cart racing, a night she'll never forget.

She thanked her parents by making them a special meal, and as the family sat around they all gave thanks for one-another before Sruthi ventured off on the next stage of her life. Sruthi was happy, and she was excited at the prospect of the enhancement of having a degree would do to her life and her goals.

Sarah and Sruthi came from two very different

upbringings and had two very different perspectives on the family unit. They had different experiences with friends, boys, hobbies, even their thoughts and opinions on school, but both wanted happiness.

These two girls were shaped by many different influences and led two very different lives. Whereas Sarah may find it acceptable to sleep in and show up late for school, Sruthi values her education and getting into a good school was a top priority. Sarah had to spend time learning to be an adult while Sruthi got to enjoy being a kid. Sarah didn't like to be around her folks, so much so that moving out of her parent's house was more important than finishing school. Sruthi, on the other hand, got to spend quality time with her family and they openly shared how much they love and supported each other.

It is very likely that these two girls with the same exact birthdays will continue living two very different lives. It's also very likely that if they ever meet, they may not enjoy each other's company- they may be too polarized from each other's life. Their standards may be the same but their boundaries are very diverse.

So what shapes our boundaries?

Heritage or culture

I remember watching Shrek with a friend of mine that

was not from the United States. Although she liked the movie, she didn't fully understand all the characters. Most of the characters in Shrek were based off a children's story, all commonly recognized in the United States. Although she thought the mice on the table that knocked over the candles were cute, she didn't quite understand that they were the 'Three Blind Mice'. The pigs were also entertaining, but why would they be huffing and puffing and trying to blow a house down? Why was there a wolf sleeping in Shrek's bed, and why was the gingerbread man upset about losing his gumdrop buttons?

It's easy for us to look at these stories and make the connection back to our childhood memories, but if these were not part of the cultural stories you grew up with then they didn't have the same meaning.

We know that when a sporting event starts and the American Flag is shown, it's customary to stand up, face the flag, remove your hat, and put your hand over your heart. You'd expect someone to start singing the National Anthem, at which point you look in awe at the flag and wait to sit down until the song is over. It's a sign of respect, it's a tradition, it's part of the culture. This may not be the same in every country and if there is a foreigner sitting during the anthem, it may not be out of disrespect, but because that's not part of their culture.

Culture and heritage impact who you are and how you

act, and although they can change, they help shape your behaviors.

Life experiences

Remember the first time you burned your hand on the stove? Remember how it felt to have the flesh on your fingers melt off and how you cried in pain? Do you remember the blisters that came after the burn, and how big it was when it filled up with liquid? It hurt to pick up anything for the next two weeks until it finally started to heal. Never again.

Life experiences can shape our boundaries. Guaranteed you are going to do your best to never touch that stove again if you can avoid it, you are going to try to put an armor around your body when you are near the stove because you know what is going to happen if you touch it again.

Do you remember when you stood up for your outlandish idea and how good you felt when it became a million-dollar idea? You knew that your gut was telling you that idea was going to be the next best thing, and sure enough- it was! You started to trust yourself more and you started believing in yourself in other areas.

Life experiences are going to shape who you are and how you respond to the world. We learn a response to actions and we make notations in our brain. *If* this happens- *then* this is the result. Now, we may not always follow the 'if/then' because we may believe there will be a different outcome, but we are still shaped by the experiences we have throughout our life.

Personalities

Think of someone you know that has a 'big personality', maybe you think of a comedian or a politician that is very strong when they come across. Conversely, think of someone who is shy and reserved. These personalities are in our DNA.

It's like the result of the Myers Briggs test. Through a series of questions, it will tell you if you're introverted or extroverted, if you're a thinker or a feeler, if you're intuitive or sensing, or if you're judging or perceiving. Within this test, there are 16 different outcomes, and this defines your personality type. This personality type gives you an idea of how you are, and it probably won't change a whole lot throughout your life. Some of the characteristics about you may be due to some of your upbringing or influences in your life, and many of them are just how you are!

My personality type is ENTP. I'm told this means 'quick, ingenious, stimulating, alert, and outspoken. I'm resourceful in solving new and challenging problems. I'm adept at generating conceptual possibilities and then analyzing them strategically. Good at reading other people. Bored by routine and apt to turn to one new interest after another' (3). That's pretty accurate!

Employers may have their employees take this test because it is an indicator of their performance, their work ethic, how they'll interact with each other, and even how to manage someone with a certain personality type.

Personalities tell a lot about us, and they can shape our boundaries. If you are more introverted then you might want to work on a project independently versus an extrovert that may want to get a big group together to collaborate.

If you are a feeler then you may be more sensitive and shy-away from situations where you could feel like you are being attacked. Thinkers, however, may welcome that level of exposure and do not take offense if someone calls them out for a behavior.

Families and friends

Sarah and Sruthi come from very different families and have very different boundaries with their lives. This influence could be religious, food, morals, values, political opinions, educational belief, and in every other area of your life. The people that are around you are going to have the biggest influence in your life. They say that you are who you surround yourself with, so choose wisely.

When we're younger we don't always have a decision when it comes to who we surround ourselves with. Mom and Dad may choose your friends or a play group on your behalf. As we grow, however, we have the ability to make choices of who we want in our inner circle. If you surround yourself with people who choose to hang out and play drinking games- then that's likely what you'll find yourself also engaging in. If you have friends that like to volunteer and go to the movies- then that's likely what you'll find yourself engaging in. And if you find that you are surrounded by entrepreneurs that are always looking to push themselves and challenge themselves and take risk- then that's likely what you'll find yourself interested in as well.

The people in your life are highly influential to yourself, and are usually a reflection of you- so choose wisely because they could be having more of an impact on you than you realize.

Where you live

If you're in a rural, urban or suburban area then you will likely have very different life experiences. You may find more kids skipping school in urban areas and the parents are less likely to find out. In rural areas, where everyone in a town knows each other, it's much harder to skip school and the teacher probably has a personal relationship with the parents.

There's a high probability you will have a lot more worldly experiences in an urban area than when you venture out into the rural areas, which will influence your standards and boundaries.

GUT

The gut is part of the body that digests your food. When the gut is in poor health it can result in high blood sugar, weight gain and high cholesterol which can then have a bigger impact on your overall health. The gut is an essential organ to your body and neglecting it can have detrimental effects.

Our gut tells us a lot of things about our body and our habits, but it also can be our instinct. Ever heard the saying 'follow your gut'? Same as when you're listening to your gut to tell you if you're eating the right foods, your gut instinct can be your guide to telling you what choice to make.

Myers Briggs may tell you if you're a thinker or a feeler, either one may have that gut instinct that is guiding decisions.

Ever had an idea that you were so excited for and couldn't stop thinking about? You would wake up in the middle of the night thinking about the idea and the potential it could have. You may have even shared this idea with some of your close friends and although they didn't have the same vision, they told you to go for it, to follow your gut.

You moved forward based off your gut instinct (and the proposal you put together) and with time and commitment you saw your idea become a million, then a multi-million dollar idea. This is usually how entrepreneurs think.

Can you imagine when computer scientists started talking about the World Wide Web? Imagine how that conversation went. 'I have this idea, that we will all be connected and be able to talk to each other through a portal. We will have unlimited access to any and all information on any topic. We will no longer need physical books or to send letters in the mail. Through this World Wide Web we will be able to send messages to each other and we will be able to access books that we can read on the screen in front of us.'

I don't know how the conversation went, but imagine it's the early 1900's, we've barely just invented the automobile, and visionaries like Paul Olet and Vannevar Bush start talking about these crazy ideas (4). If they hadn't, or if others hadn't shared and executed on that vision then maybe our world today would look quite different. Think about before the automobile, before airplanes, before television, before color tv, before songs went on record- all of those ideas were a vision, a gut instinct, and history would look a lot different if their gut hadn't been followed.

The gut is powerful and sometimes it needs to be your guide. If it's telling you something isn't right in your life, then it probably means you need to make a change. If that old fling of yours comes into town and calls you up and you think there's more to the lunch than simply food, then it's probably best to decline that offer.

There are a lot of factors that come into play when we start to look at what influences boundaries. These boundaries and standards may change over time. There is no 'one answer' or 'one way' of doing something, but know that they are largely impacted by a culmination of influences and circumstances over a persons lifetime.

Chapter 7: Why do we Need Boundaries?

Everyone that has ever climbed Mt. Everest has had to prepare for the trek. No one happens to be walking by the mountain and decides to scale it the next day. Unpreparedness is just not possible. At 29,028 feet, Everest graces the world as the tallest mountain. Having flown by the mountain range that includes Everest at 35,000 feet in the air and seeing the tips of the mountain tops pierce through the clouds was such an impressive and majestic sight unlike anything I had ever experienced. To think that someone would actually climb to those heights is impressive.

At the peaks of those mountains, the spikey tips are covered in snow and ice. The temperatures average between -19 to -36 degrees Fahrenheit (5), a temperature that if unprepared will cause hypothermia to even the world's best climber. The change in altitude is nothing we experience in our daily lives. It takes practice and experience and often the assistance of special equipment to help mitigate the environmental conditions and acclimate our lungs.

It's preparedness.

At almost 30,000 feet in the air anything can happen, and if you begin to climb without a plan, then your chances of success are minimized. Failure is almost a given.

Of course you would plan, right? Is that what you're thinking to yourself now?

There's no way you would take on such a journey and not train your body, train your lungs, buy the proper equipment, map your ascent, have enough food, or bring shelter- it's preposterous! All of those things will keep you more comfortable, able to withstand the elements, and ultimately keep you alive.

Approaching the climb to that mountain should be no different than your approach to your life. If you walk in without a map and a plan, if you have to deal with every situation as it arises without knowing how to handle it, then good luck getting to where you're going, and I hope you enjoy the unnecessary bumps that could have been avoided.

Having a map and a plan doesn't mean your trek always goes as anticipated, but it does mean you're prepared. Hiking Mt. Everest, the climbers have to anticipate many different scenarios before setting out on their journey. What if they experience a blizzard? How will they stay warm? What if it rains? What if they need a knife or other equipment? What if they get lost from the planned ascent route? What about a backup battery for their phone? Will their phone even work, would another form of communication be better?

What if they run out of food? What if they get separated from their group? What if, what if, what if.

Though they may not be able to map out every situation it's in their best interest to preplan and anticipate scenarios in advance, because once they're in a situation, it might be too late to deal with it. They'll know for the next time, that's assuming they make it back down to the base camp.

There are going to be loads of unknowns as you go through your life, and you can walk into an entirely new situation armed with boundaries to keep you protected.

So why do you need to have boundaries in your life?

Reduce anxiety

Think about a time you had to give a speech to your boss' boss or even the CEO and you weren't prepared. Do you remember the anxiety you had leading up to it since you didn't have a plan on what you were going to speak about?

Maybe your boss asked you a week ago, and instead of focusing on the speech and making it a priority you had 'other things' that took precedence.

Or maybe, your boss asked you 30 minutes ago, and

even though you knew it wasn't enough time to prepare, you said yes anyhow.

If you had only used that week to prepare and not prioritized everything else ahead of this meeting, or if you had only told your boss you would need an extra day, then you might not have sweaty palms and wet armpits right now. You knew that going to happy hour last night was a bad idea, but you went even though you knew in your mind you needed that time to prepare. You knew in your mind that you were setting yourself up for not putting your best foot forward by agreeing to present with zero time to prepare. You knew this could be a pivotal moment in your career if you were able to show the CEO your knowledge, passion and presentation skills, but it could also be equally detrimental.

You blew your boundary of not going out for happy hour. You blew your boundary of not communicating to your boss if you felt you were being set up for failure. A little bit of boundaries here could have reduced your anxiety quite a bit and you could be sitting calmly with cool hands and dry pits.

Make life easier

Have you ever tried to open a can without a can opener? You find a knife and start stabbing the can. You make a few dents, and in the end you throw the can AND the knife away because they're both useless now. If only you had a can opener, or bought a can that had a pop top. Life is easier when you're prepared.

Boundaries make life easier because they prepare you for how to operate in a situation.

Save time

Imagine if every time a company got an invoice they had to establish a process for payment. Instead of sitting down and coming up with a flowchart and assigning roles and responsibilities, the company decided to come up with a different process each time. Imagine the amount of time wasted and the number of errors that company would need to sift through. It's good to have process and routine.

Think about if this was your own life and every time you went on a date, every time there was a new friend in your life, every time you got a new job, every night when you went to bed, every morning when you woke up you were having to establish a new expectation for yourself- this would be a lot of wasted time.

Your boundaries are your expectations for yourself and if you don't adhere to them then you are likely disappointing yourself and wasting yourself a lot of unnecessary time.

Stay in a more positive space

If you've made the conscientious decision to be positive and you establish the proper boundaries, then you'll find yourself in a more consistent positive space, regardless of what is happening around you.

I will never forget living through the Coronavirus crisis of 2020. The negativity was rampant, and I remained surprisingly positive. I almost felt like a unicorn throwing up on people because I just found so much good in everything! I was gifted time to get things organized, to grow my business. My first book, "RESET", had just launched and I could focus on marketing. I recorded my audible book, I finished my on-line course material, I wrote this book.

I reconnected with friends I hadn't spoken to in a while. My cat and I seemed to improve our relationship. I got to focus on tending to my face and reducing my scars I had for years. I even got to watch some movies which I never took the time to do!

I still had bills, my income had been compromised, I had to social distance from the rest of the world, but I made that decision to remain positive.

Think about a time that you did something that you know you shouldn't have. Did it go against your moral compass or your values? Were you disappointed in yourself? It may be sheer disappointment in ourselves for why we get into a negative space, or you get frustrated because you're constantly reinventing the wheel, or you feel overwhelmed, but when you are prepared then you minimize these responses of feeling down on yourself.

Choosing positivity, establishing the right boundaries, and holding yourself to them will keep you in a more positive space- you won't disappoint yourself!

Improve self-esteem

When you establish boundaries in your life, and follow through, then you are ensuring your needs are met.

My clients will often tell me that they are upset over a situation. Maybe they went on a date with someone and ended up spending the night. Or maybe they drank too much the night before. Or maybe they didn't speak up in a meeting when they knew they had valuable information to contribute. My question to them is always, did you establish your boundary?

Did you communicate to your date that you didn't want to spend the night? Why didn't you leave when you knew you wanted to? Why did you open the bottle of wine or not stop after 2 drinks? What stopped you from speaking up?

The conclusion they always arrive at is there had been no boundaries either established or enforced.

Each time, the end result was the same: disappointment. This disappointment would lead to low self-esteem and often even depression.

Think of how much better you would feel if you set a plan for yourself and you followed through. You said you were going to speak up for yourself and you did.

Setting boundaries ensures your needs are met, which ultimately raises your self-esteem. You are being true to you, and you make sure others treat you with the same level of respect.

Reduce surprises

If you are prepared, if you know how you are going to respond, then you significantly reduce surprises in your life. Think about those hikers. If they were not prepared for a blizzard and they encountered one, then it would be a rather unpleasant surprise to say the least! In fact, it could have a very negative impact on their overall journey. If they caught hypothermia because they were cold and wet, then not only might they have to turn around, but they also risk death.

AI (Artificial Intelligence) is becoming a massive

industry. It's machines learning patterns and behaviors, and this learning can be applied across many industries. Think about the management of your credit card activity. AI is used to detect unusual activity patterns to help keep you safe. If it detects there's something unusual then you get a call, an email, or maybe even a text notifying you of suspicious activity. Much better getting a call to validate suspicious activity versus getting a bill with thousands of dollars in charges from a Target hundreds of miles from you.

Boundaries are like artificial intelligence. When you go outside of them then a red flag is raised or they catch you off guard. This is why your self-esteem can be compromised. If you haven't clearly established boundaries or you don't hold yourself to them, then that alarm goes off and you don't feel good about it.

AI anticipates what's coming, it knows what to expect. It doesn't like surprises. Same with boundaries. When you have them in place then you're making the decision to reduce the surprise factor in your life.

Improve your relationships with others

When two people know what boundaries to stay within then they'll enhance their overall relationship. Imagine if you had a friend that came over uninvited and always at the worst time, or would stay too late when you really wanted to go to sleep. Perhaps they put you down for your political beliefs, use the rest of the toilet paper and not replace the roll, or even come over and drink all your beer and never bring any. Could you imagine this person as a friend? Maybe you even have someone that comes to mind!

If you have a bedtime, if you want there to be toilet paper available when you use the restroom, if you don't want to always pay for someone else to drink all your beer- then guess what, you need boundaries!

When there is a mutual respect of boundaries, imagine how much better this relationship would be. You wouldn't curse his name when you sat on the john needing toilet paper when it was too late to realize there was none there!

Boundaries ensure needs are being met, and once you know, then you can stay within the lines and enjoy each other's company! And if they know but don't respect your boundaries then you know what you need to do, right?

Play offense rather than defense

Ever tried playing a game without a playbook? A coach without a playbook, without a strategy would be fired. It's an expectation of any owner of a team to have a coach that is able to call out plays, make the most of his team's abilities, navigate the field, and ultimately win the game.

Boundaries put you in the offensive position because you know how to play the game. That playbook, those moves, those tactics are your boundaries.

Without a proper strategy, you are running the ball on hope. You are hoping you have a blocker, you are hoping you have someone to pass the ball to, you are hoping you are a faster runner. At that point, you're playing on hope, and you're probably playing without a coach because no coach would just throw you in the game unprepared.

When you're following strategy, when you study the opposition and know what to expect, when you have a connection with the players on the field and you know where and when to throw the ball- you will be a lot more successful than just playing on hope.

Your boundaries are your offensive strategy.

Conserve energy

Have you ever watched a boxing match where one boxer allows her opponent to get in jabs and punches while she diligently covers her face and her body and blocks the punches? Doesn't make for an overly interesting fight, in fact you wonder when she's going to wake up and start punching back. Was she scared? Why wasn't she doing anything? The opponent goes round after round using up all the energy in her wheelhouse, it's clear she's running out of steam. Finally, in the 5th round, the boxer that blocked the punches and conserved her energy opened up in the last 30 seconds and with one blow to the face, the tired boxer that went 5 rounds with her opponent, landed 200 punches, fell flat to the ground and lost the fight.

What appeared to the crowd as a timid fighter actually proved to be a strategic play. She allowed her opponent to hit a level of exhaustion before making her own move.

The winner of the fight had a strategy, and that was to conserve her energy and unleash when the timing felt right.

When you don't set boundaries, then you are the fighter that is constantly jabbing and punching. I think back to my own life and how exhausted I was to deal with every situation as it arose. I had a few boundaries in place, but I didn't take the time to assess all areas of my life. If I had, then I would have had more energy because I wouldn't have always been fighting and reinventing the wheel.

Get respect

When the President enters a room the people stand to their feet. Same as a wedding. People don't stand when the wedding party walks down the aisle, but when that bride steps out into focus, people rise.

Why?

It's a sign of respect. Same is true with boundaries. If you respect me, then you will respect my boundary. If I say NO, then you should respect me by not pushing that boundary.

Ever heard of a delinquent referred to as 'not respecting authority'? That's because there are laws that govern the land (boundaries), and when someone does not abide by them then they are not respecting the laws that the authorities put in place.

You are your authority. You make your own laws. You govern your land. And if someone does not follow, then they are not showing you respect. On the other hand, and we know there is a larger majority that do abide by your governance, and those that do are actually showing you respect.

I don't think I've ever walked up to a random stranger and run my fingers through their hair. I know for me personally, that would be a boundary crossed, I don't want your random hands in my hair if I don't give you permission!

Someone adhering to your boundaries is like the guests standing as that bride walks down the aisle, it's a sign of respect.

But, respect is also a two-way street. If you don't hold yourself to your own boundary, then you cannot expect that someone else is going to adhere to it. If you don't show others respect, then reduces your chances that someone will adhere to yours (or at least have respect for you as a person). We'll dig deeper in that in an upcoming chapter, but know that respect isn't a one-way street.

~~~~

We need boundaries in our life because they give us an overall improved experience as we go through life. You'll have more energy, more time, and a better quality of life. You'll reduce the number of unwanted surprises, you'll improve your self-esteem, you'll improve your relationships. You get to play life on the offense, rather than on the defense. You'll get the respect from others and from yourself when you abide by the guidelines and boundaries you put in place.

If you don't put boundaries in place then you are leaving life up to chance, and no one wants to chance sitting on the toilet wondering if there will be toilet paper or not.

~~~~

Let's dig into each type of boundary and start to form

your thoughts and opinions about each one as it pertains to you. Remember your standards and how you want others to view you. Think about where you have angst in your life and where you know something isn't right. Think about where you are not at your very happiest and start to see if some of the boundaries stand out to you. Write some of these down so you can see them on paper or write them in the book. If you have an 'ah-ha' moment, then I want you to email me and let me know, because I know this is going to open your eyes.

It may seem like a lot to digest, but you are already doing these things in your daily life in some capacity. You may not have formally assessed what your boundaries are, you're simply doing them. These should be natural, you should be able to navigate through the world and not have to always stop and think. If you have any contention in your life, then there is something that needs to be addressed. You should always be choosing happy. If you are not happy, then something is off.

Why do most of us go to the doctor (besides a general checkup)? It's because there is something wrong. We don't go to a specialist because we want to say HI, we go because there is something that hurts, doesn't feel right, or we have odd symptoms we just can't make sense of. It is the same in your life. If you are feeling hurt, something isn't right. If you are anything but happy then it's time to really take a hard look at your life.

You wouldn't start driving to Argentina without a map or GPS, so don't you think you should have one to navigate your life? You know from your standards that your happiness is the goal, you want to be respected, honest, trustworthy, easy to communicate with, and you can have all of those things if you just have a guide. These boundaries are to protect you and help you grow as a person. There are different boundaries you will use for different types of situations. If you become aware of what boundaries are, stay in tune with your feelings and keep trucking towards your standards, then you are going to be unstoppable!

Boundaries are everywhere, and if you are able to breathe then you have some boundaries in your life. They're unavoidable, they're necessary. They govern your life and let you and others know how to work with you. *Boundaries are power, and if you don't realize that, then you are sitting on an untapped goldmine!*

Chapter 8: Material & Time Boundaries

Every day of your life you are dealing with time and things. You probably have an alarm clock you wake up to and things you need to get you ready for the day. You may go into an office or maybe you need to get the kids up for school (or both). You need to get things ready to start your day and you hope you made sure to put your phone on the charger the night before so it is sufficiently charged. If not, you need to remember to bring a charger.

It is inevitable that time and material objects come into play during your day.

Material Boundaries

Think about the possessions you have in your life, the material things you can physically touch. Have you ever thought about the boundaries you have around them? Would you put a cup with no lid next to your electronics? Do you allow your telephone at the dinner table? Do you allow your cat to jump on the counter? Do you allow a television in your bedroom, and if you do, does it have to go off at a certain time?

How about what you're willing to lend to people.

Do you have any qualms with lending money? Do you have any stipulations around lending money, or maybe this is something you avoid all together?

Would you let someone borrow your lawn mower? If so, do you expect it to be returned later that day? Do you expect the gas to be replaced in the mower? If there wasn't gas in it when it was returned, would you say something then? Would you let the person borrow your lawn mower again? Would you give a stipulation the next time before it was borrowed, or would you go through this whole scenario again and not have it meet your expectations as it did the first time?

How about your toothbrush? Would you let your friend borrow it? How about your spouse? What if someone used it and you didn't want them to- would you throw it away?

Would you say something in all these situations, or would you merely leave it to fate? Many people will leave it to fate because they are people pleasers or they feel uncomfortable with confrontation. They'll keep their thoughts and opinions inside, let them fester, share them with someone that they can complain to, and let it tear them up causing discontent.

Are you consistent with your messaging and establishing boundaries, and do people even know what your boundaries are? If someone borrows money, do you tell them they need to repay you or do you just assume they will. Let's say they never repay you, do you take any ownership in that if you never told them they needed to pay you back? Maybe they thought they were given a gift, so it's up to you to be very clear on the expectations and your rules. Otherwise, this leads you down a path of anger and frustration because you both had two different ideas of how the money should have been handled, but because it was never discussed it was left to the individual's interpretation.

We'll talk about communication in an upcoming chapter, but think about these situations and how you would respond. What is the role you play in determining the outcome? Are you an active participant in the direction your life goes, or do you just complain to your friends when it doesn't go your way?

Day-in and day-out you are constantly dealing with material boundaries. Unless you live you in a box with nothing in it, then you deal with these boundaries. Think about what is in your space and the rules you have around them. You come in contact with these things every day, they're what you see, what you hold, they are all around you. It's important to become cognizant of them not just as 'things' in your space, but start to assess the rules, the purpose, the boundaries you have around them.

Time Boundaries

Ever met someone that was consistently 30 minutes late? Maybe that person is you. Is time just a suggestion, or do you hold yourself to arriving at some place at the specified time? Maybe it varies.

If there is a meeting for work do you plan to be there on-time? If it's a party, do you prefer to show up 30 minutes late because you don't want to be the first to arrive?

Maybe you have an early bedtime. You've made sleep a priority in your life and if you are late to the party then you either stay for a shorter amount of time, or you arrive first so you can leave first. Or, maybe you don't like crowds and you know the later on it is into the evening the more crowded it gets. Maybe this is a party for a good friend and you know that your presence is needed throughout the entire time and you had better be there on-time. Or, perhaps this party is for an acquaintance and you want to show up just to show your face and drop off a bottle of wine.

So many decisions and options, and there's no one answer for how long you should stay or when you should arrive to the party- it all depends.

- You're not staying past 9pm.
- You're not arriving first.
- You're not going to be late.

- You're not going to be last.
- You're not staying more than an hour.
- You're committed to staying the whole time.
- You're just going to go until you feel like leaving. When you're done, you'll go!

There are loads of ways to slice and dice your decision. Behind each one of those decisions is a reasoning. What goal are you trying to achieve determines how you spend your time. Once you know that, then you put boundaries in place.

I spent years never getting enough sleep. I would stay up late and get up early, and if I got 5 hours of sleep it was a good night. This may have been easier when I was in my 20's, but when I got into my 30's I really started to feel the strain. My energy levels were completely different in my 30's, and I was finding it harder to focus and be productive in the middle of the day. I finally decided that getting a good night's rest was going to be a standard in my life and I built boundaries around that. If I needed to stay up later one night, then I would shift my morning workout to the evening so I could make sure to get in my sleep. I would shift my schedule around the fact that I chose sleep as a priority in my life, and I started to feel better about my energy and ability to focus during the day. I also noticed some other great health benefits like reduced lines on my face.

Think of time boundaries like time management. You

lay out your schedule for the day and you readjust based off priorities.

Like material boundaries (and all of the other boundaries), you need to communicate these as well. If sleep has become a priority then make sure your significant other is aware so you both are on the same page when it comes to expectations.

I think of my mother and her morning routine when I was growing up. I knew that Mom was going to work out in the morning then followed by her daily meditation with the Lord. I never questioned what Mom was doing in the morning, I knew what to expect because it was her routine. We always knew when Mom wasn't feeling well because she would skip her workout (which was few-and-far-between). Her consistency with her time boundaries created a daily structure that we worked around. We knew not to bother her during a certain hour (unless there was something urgent) because she was faithful and consistent with her time.

Aligning time and material boundaries with your standards will help create consistency and predictability. If your standard is to be on-time for meetings then it might mean you leave your previous meeting 5 minutes beforehand so you can make your next meeting on-time.

Time and material boundaries are an unavoidable part of life. They help dictate your moves throughout the day. There are 'things' everywhere we look and every place we touch. The sun and moon keep us aligned when it's daytime or nighttime, and our biological clocks are on their own agenda. Wherever you look, you are having to make decisions about material and time boundaries, they play a major piece in how we structure our lives.

Chapter 9: Physical and Sexual Boundaries

Physical and sexual boundaries can vary widely and are largely influenced by culture, upbringing and comfort. Boundaries crossed in these spaces have the potential to be weighed more heavily than borrowing someone's toothbrush or showing up late for a meeting. It's important to be aware of not only your own boundaries but it is imperative to be in tune with other's boundaries, as the repercussions of crossing them might bring unintended results.

We're talking about the space and contact in between you and another. Think of this like state boundaries. There is a distinct line between two states, and on each side there two different governing laws. In 2014, the use of marijuana was legalized in the state of Colorado. Directly to the East, in the state of Kansas, however, it was illegal to use marijuana even for medicinal purposes. If you were on a hike and had marijuana in your possession and you crossed from Colorado into Kansas then you went from carrying a legal substance to carrying an illegal substance. This could result in an arrest and maybe even jail time.

It's important to understand the governing laws around physical and sexual boundaries because there can be consequences if boundaries are crossed.

Physical boundaries

Are you a hugger or more of a handshake kind of
person? Do you care if someone touches your hair, or
do you prefer people keep their hands to themselves?
Are you one of those people that touch other people
when you talk? Do you care if people touch you when
they talk? Is there a distance that is too close to talk to
someone? Would 5 inches from your face feel too close?
When you stand in line, is there an appropriate amount
of space you should leave between you and the person
in front of you?

How about noise. Is there a level of music that is too
loud? Is it different when you're driving than when
you're in your house? Do you play the music more
loudly when you're driving down the road than when
you're pulling into your neighborhood?

How do you feel about wearing a swimsuit? Does it
vary depending on the company? Would you wear the
same swimsuit around your family that you would
with coworkers? Would you wear a different swimsuit
for your spouse than for your children? What about
the other parents in the neighborhood- would it be a
different suit for them as well, and maybe one that they
would deem 'appropriate'? Or, are you
unapologetically you and you wear whatever you want
whenever you want?

A physical boundary is that invisible line around you

that governs your space. This may be physical, audible or aromatic, but it's anything entering your space. It's anything you interact with, and it's not a one-way street. It's how things interact with you and it's how you interact with the world and with others.

You may think it's ok to play your music at a certain volume, but what about your neighbors or people in your own home. Is it acceptable to play the drums outside of your house at midnight?

What determines acceptable?

Cultural norms have a large influence on physical boundaries.

I have traveled the globe and I can attest that personal space varies country to country (even region to region). I spent a couple of months in Delhi, India and had such an incredible time and such an eye-opening experience. Space was one of the first differences I felt. I don't know if the distancing between people seemed to be less because the country had a much higher population than the United States, but I certainly experienced some discomfort when people were standing inches behind me, instead of a comfortable foot or more. To them, this was the norm, for me I felt like if you couldn't raise your hand comfortably to catch your own sneeze then you were entirely too close.

I took a trip to the magnificent Taj Mahal, and it is just

as majestic as it looked in photos. As we arrived in Agra, India, our mouths dropped as we approached the white mausoleum. The symmetry was breathtaking. The eye started at the long, narrow water way that led up to the ivory-white marble building crowned with perfectly white domes that pierced the sky. It earned every right to hold the prestigious title of being one of the 7 New Wonders of the World.

As we got out of the taxi we found ourselves in a flood of vibrant color. Most of the women were draped in traditional sarees which were all robust in color. The color popped against the massive white building behind them, truly a spectacular site. As we made our way to enter the Taj Mahal we noticed there was a line that wrapped nearly around the building. We made our way to the end and started to notice immediately that this was not a line we were used to standing in.

There were people lining up that thought 'cutting' in line was acceptable. They would insert themselves into the line where they wanted to stand. I've always gone to the back of the line and started there, but apparently you can choose where you'd like to start. There were some people that would react and call the person out, and there were others that would permit it to happen. Blew my mind.

There were others that would be standing at some point in the line and maybe when they thought people weren't paying attention, they would run over to another place in line closer to the entrance. I'm not sure if they thought they were doing a magic trick, but I certainly could see them. Same response, some people would react and call the person out, and others that would permit it to happen. This didn't happen once, but there seemed to be these characters everywhere. It was almost like watching a video game.

Physical boundaries, to include behavior, vary greatly. India isn't the only country that has a closer proximity comfort zone. I've certainly experienced this in China, Israel and Italy. If someone tries to stand in line in the United States and pull those 'games' or stand three inches behind the person in front of them then they are very likely to say something. I know I've turned around given someone a look for standing too close.

It's cultural, it's personal, and it drives our behavior and responses.

Standing or speaking too close may make you feel entirely uncomfortable, but how about wearing a tiny swimsuit in front of the neighbors? Would that make you flinch, or are you perfectly comfortable? Does your music volume vary on the time of day or if you're at your house or in your car? These are decisions we are constantly making and boundaries that are driving our lives.

Like the state line, physical boundaries are important because they tell you what is acceptable in the space you govern. But, you are not the only governing law, you have to be aware of everyone else that is in your space or there could be a backlash and dirty looks when you wait in line entirely too close to the person in front of you.

Sexual Boundaries

Sexual boundaries help you to know the what, when, where, how and with whom. This applies for anyone, married or not, and it's important to know where you stand and where the other person stands. If you cross someone's sexual boundary then this could have unintended results. Physical touch is a very vulnerable and personal subject. There is an amount of trust that is involved and if boundaries are overstepped then trust can be lost and it can have disastrous results.

What's appropriate on a first date? Is fidelity important? Is flirting with someone when you're in a committed relationship with someone else an appropriate behavior? Is kissing in public ok? Are you ok with watching movies with sexually explicit scenes? Would you be comfortable watching these movies with your spouse but not with your kids? How do you feel about wearing see-through clothing? Would you be offended if someone was showing their privates through their outfit?

Sexual boundaries tend to be a lot more rigid. You may

be flexible or more lenient in your response to the volume of your neighbor's music, but if your neighbor came over and tried to sleep with your spouse then the response would be drastically different.

A noise violation with the county may look like a warning or a fine if it happens on repeated occasions. A sexual violation, however, has much more severe penalties. There are rules around age, consent, infidelity, bestiality, indecent exposure, exploitation and molestation (to name a few). The results could be life changing and could easily result in serving a prison sentence.

Sexual boundaries are not just only knowing the law and your rights, but they dictate how we allow people into our space. Not all are legally driven. You may be promiscuous and your boundary is set differently than someone who wants to wait for marriage to engage in sexual activity. There's a wide spectrum, but it's highly crucial to be informed and clear in your boundaries to protect you from getting into an unwanted situation, at any level.

Physical and sexual boundaries are sensitive subjects as they can be highly personal. Know your rights, know your boundaries, and be clear. Unclear boundaries are only going to add confusion and lead to disappointment or unintended outcomes. Be aware of cultural norms and standards, what might be acceptable in one area may have severe penalties elsewhere.

If you have set high standards in your life then building the right boundaries should be the easy piece and have a higher probability of keeping you out of unwanted situations. If the boundaries you have previously set no longer serve you, then redefine them and implement new ones.

Chapter 10: Intellectual and Emotional Boundaries

Intellectual and Emotional boundaries can be felt. Being in tune with your feelings, being cognizant of how you and others interpret situations is important to both types of boundaries. They can keep you from getting into situations where you get emotionally charged or making a statement that could just flat out be offensive without you knowing.

Intellectual Boundaries

Intellectual boundaries don't measure intellect, per se, but rather thoughts and ideas. These include when to insert your opinion or when you should stay quiet. What might be the 'right time' to say something, what is respectful versus disrespectful. It's understanding timing and what is appropriate and when.

Ever heard someone start talking about politics and you thought 'man, they really shouldn't go there'. Maybe it was in a setting outside of the home with someone you know or on social media but surely it's going to misalign with someone's opinion.

Then, there's that guy in the office, and yes- he's nice, but he can be really obnoxious when talking about talking about his cars and vacations. Not everyone has the wealth to afford them, and it's starting to really rub people the wrong way. Times are really tough for some of the people in the office, and it seems like this guy is bragging. He may not realize it, but that's how it comes off. Even if he's really smart, the fact that he's offending people in the office and making them feel uncomfortable trumps the fact that he's really good at his job. People are left with the impression that he's a jerk, and he may have zero awareness that his boundaries are not dialed in to his surroundings.

Sounds like this guy needs to be a bit more in tune with what message he's putting out and the people he's around. Whereas he may have friends that are all well off and live a lavish lifestyle, it might not be ok to flaunt your wealth around people that are not in the same position.

Could you imagine if your boss came up to you and said 'I make significantly more money than you? That is usually the case, but certainly not a conversation that is appropriate to have.

Intellectual boundaries, then, are knowing what to say and when to say it.

Topics like sex, politics, religion, money can be sensitive subjects people typically have very distinct and widely varied opinions about them. They are also very personal, so they can be rather offensive if they do not align with YOUR beliefs. Usually it's best to keep those conversations for the right time and place, which might be with closer friends or family, or you might just want to keep some of them to yourself all together. Even when you think you know someone's opinion or boundary on one of these topics, you could be greatly surprised if you are even slightly wrong.

Intellectual boundaries are thoughts and ideas and knowing when it is appropriate to bring them up. If children are in the room then there might be a different level of 'adult conversation' that should be kept for after they go to bed or leave the room. If you know something sensitive just happened in someone's world then you should probably be respectful and not say things that would cause that person discomfort.

Having intellectual boundaries might keep you out of situations that could get uncomfortable quickly. When you speak up and it's not appropriate, usually these conversations don't go over well and they could tarnish your overall reputation. If you are looking for respect, it's good to know what and when it's appropriate to insert your thoughts and ideas, especially on sensitive topics.

The old adage, 'think before you speak' certainly comes into play here. If you are talking about a topic that is debatable, assess your surroundings before you speak, or just keep it to yourself all together. Might you be saying something that is likely to be offensive to someone? This too may vary, and you may need to know the person better before you can assess if they may take offense to your comment.

When I was growing up I was very sensitive about comments pertaining to my height. It boiled down to my own insecurity and I was very defensive when anyone said anything. Now, my mental boundaries block comments and I have learned to accept them as curiosity versus mockery or judgement. I'm not everyone, and there may be many women out there that do not like comments about their height. When I was feeling down about the comments, my Dad always would say "Would you rather be 6 feet tall or 5 feet tall?". Maybe that made me feel a little better, but if he had said that around someone that was 5 feet tall, how would that have made them feel?

Knowing your company and their boundaries, knowing social norms (like not approaching your employee and telling them you make more than them), and being in tune with the appropriateness of the situation will help you build strong intellectual boundaries, which also comes with a greater chance of garnering respect.

Emotional Boundaries

Emotional boundaries can be tricky, since they are tied to our feelings. Typically, people want to 'feel good' or make others 'feel good' so they will often act based off this sense.

Emotional boundaries make up a protective layer that exists between you and another person, place or thing. Think about your space, only yours. Now, add another person into the picture, and any decisions, feelings, emotions that involve this other person are emotional boundaries.

This might include blaming others for your actions, or blaming yourself for theirs. It's acting based on emotion, rather than fact. It's allowing other's emotions and feelings to dictate your response, or putting someone else's needs above your own.

Emotional boundaries can keep you feeling guilty, feeling sorry for yourself, or determine where you place blame in a situation. Do you take responsibility for your actions or do you blame them on others? Emotional boundaries tap into feelings and are very powerful. Knowing when to use the right boundaries is the key, because we are constantly in each other's emotional space.

Ever seen someone that's 30 years old that lives at home? They're perfectly capable of living on their own and their mom & dad have no health issues. Dad's ready for their son to be out of the house, but mom feels guilty for never having been around during the child's early stages. Mom was off working on her career and the son never lets her forget just how many recitals she missed and how many soccer games she wasn't able to make. Poor mom feels so guilty for not showing up when her son was a kid, that she allows him to stay, and stay rent free.

Mom is now trying to make up for lost time, or so she believes. She cooks, she cleans, she gives her son money, there is almost nothing her son does for himself. The guilt of being an absent mother is so gut wrenching that she will do almost anything to try to mend the relationship, and she believes that's allowing him to live as an adult with no responsibilities. She is enabling his behavior.

Her husband confronts her at times, because he's ready to have an empty house, and he thinks his son needs to learn to be an adult. Every time he says something, his wife breaks down in tears and he backs off. He doesn't want to lose his marriage over the guilt his wife feels over their son, so he chooses to pick his battles. He knows others are judging him, his buddies will throw in comments when they're on the golf course, and he tries to laugh it off. Inside, he's not doing well, he's emotionally drained at the situation. He's even lost respect for his son for not stepping into the role of a man. His own father would never have allowed that behavior, and he equates his success to his father pushing him to be independent. He's doing a disservice to his son and he knows it. In his own way, he too is enabling his son's behavior.

Dad wants his wife back, he sees her getting more

wrapped up in her son's life every day, coddling him. They haven't gone on a proper date in years, and he misses what they once had. He's become used to the situation, but that doesn't mean he likes it. He finds more enjoyment these days at work, especially since someone new at work has taken interest in him. 'She's only a coworker', he tells himself, but the reality is that he likes the attention that he never seems to get any more at home.

Tough situation.

Lots of emotional boundaries are being pushed here, and it's clear to anyone looking in at the situation that something needs to be addressed.

- Son blames mom for not being present during his childhood
- Son is taking advantage of his mother's guilt
- Mom is acting out of guilt
- Mom feels responsible for fixing the situation from decades past
- Dad is not responding out of fear
- Dad feels guilty for not pushing for independence
- Mom & Dad are enabling their son to do nothing with his life
- Mom & Dad can both feel the impact in their marriage because they do not align and can't seem to talk about the situation without emotion

- Dad is filling emotional needs with a female coworker

Emotions can be tricky because many times we lead with our heart. It can be hard to separate ourselves or put up appropriate boundaries especially when it comes to people we're close with and care for. Mom & Dad needed to have a discussion about their son and talk facts. Dad feels neglected, mom feels guilt, son takes advantage. Recognizing and discussing is exactly what this family needs to get back on track. The emotional boundaries either don't exist or they over stepped, and the relationship has suffered because of it.

Remember being sick when you were a young kid and your mom would tend to you? She would bring you soup and crackers, bring you a cold washcloth for your warm head, and she'd let you watch as many movies as wanted. You weren't responsible for anything.

This went on for a good couple of days and, although you were sick, you rather enjoyed the pampering. You didn't have to do chores, go to school, or put your dishes in the dishwasher. You could do whatever you wanted, and mom did all the 'hard stuff'.

You started to feel better at some point, but you thought to yourself, 'if I can keep this up, mom will keep letting me watch movies and skip school.' Seemed like a good idea! But, Mom knew better, and she could tell when you were starting to play games.

She wasn't going to be your full-time master, she was just helping you get better.

"I need just one more day, I still feel sick."

"Let me feel your head. Nope. You're not sick. Get up, get dressed, you're headed to school."

"But, Mom!"

"No, buts, you're fine."

And just like that, your days in the king's seat were over and life had resumed.

Mom certainly had emotions tied to her actions, but since her son was a young boy she felt it was her motherly responsibility to take care of her son. She wanted him to feel better, and the faster he got better the faster she could get back to work. Her company frowned upon working from home, so she wanted to get back as quickly as she could.

She was no fool, though, she knew when her son had started to 'act sick' and take advantage of the situation, and that's where she drew the line. She was ok with taking care of her son when he was sick, but she would not allow him to skip school and watch movies if he was perfectly well. Not on her watch!

Yes, there were decisions based on emotions, but there

were also strong boundaries in place so Mom was not taken advantage of.

It's not bad to act on emotions but knowing when your emotional boundary is being taken advantage of or when you are crossing is a line is what you need to be able to discern and be prepared to act appropriately.

Have you ever had an employee work for you that you were always very cautious to give feedback to because he would get upset and defensive? As the boss you want to help groom and develop your employees, but this one always felt he was right and just flat out couldn't take constructive criticism.

One day you get called into Human Resource (HR) because your employee has filed a complaint of 'bullying'. This employee felt that you, although you were the boss, were bullying when you provided feedback (he even asked for advice at times and you did, not knowing he was stewing on the inside and about to explode).

The discussion with HR came to you as a surprise because in the three years you had been this employee's boss, nothing had ever been said about bullying or hard feelings. In fact, you thought the relationship was good and you tried to be more cautious with your words because you knew this employee had weak emotional boundaries.

An investigation gets conducted on you and you had to go back through years of emails and texts, not just to this employee, but with all your colleagues. You run across a text message from this person stating you were the best boss in the world, and now here was a complaint. If you believed in your heart that you were bullying, then this would have been an easier pill to swallow, but you had not changed your opinion or approach with the employee. After the investigation was completed the results were given to you. Inconclusive; you had not treated this employee differently than any other employee.

It became a rather awkward situation for you, because the company takes these offenses very seriously and your boss had to be brought into the loop. You realized, however, that this employee has always demonstrated weak emotional boundaries and he was always quick to get upset, defensive, and it was a coin toss to which personality he was bringing to the office on any given day. In the end, you had to realize there was more going on with this employee and it wasn't really about you, but there were things you could learn and do differently next time.

People with weak emotional boundaries tend to knee-jerk react and are not as in control of their emotions. You see this type of overreaction when someone reacts poorly to constructive criticism, blaming other people for their problems, letting others manipulate their feelings, being taken advantage of, letting their emotions fester inside and waiting for them to bubble over.

This is not to say if someone dies and you respond by crying that you have weak emotional boundaries. In fact, any emotion where you are faced with heartache from a loss may very well take time to grieve. It is perfectly understandable that after a big loss or life changing event that it will take some time to get back on track, but it's not advisable to stay in that state. If you are constantly living in the past then you will keep yourself from moving forward. Holding on to that unhappiness will ultimately weigh you down, but grieving for a period of time is understandable.

I love going to Vegas. I enjoy getting dressed up, going dancing, walking the strip, seeing shows, visiting the M&M store (that's my personal favorite), climbing the wall in the Twin Peaks restaurant, I love so many things about Vegas. I have a tough time gambling though. I like the idea of winning money, but I also hate the idea of losing money. I'm such a frugal person by nature (that may be an understatement in some contexts), that I don't know that the thrill of rolling the dice supersedes the anxiety I get when I lose money. I may take a $20 and give it a go, but I hate that feeling of losing money, I'd much rather spend it on something I know I would benefit from (like a pound of M&Ms).

I know that I do not have strong emotional boundaries

around gambling. Some people can distance their feelings from putting their money on the table and watching it be taken away, but I know that I'm not as strong there. I know I should avoid putting myself in these situations, or put clear boundaries in place, because it doesn't naturally settle well with me and I know that. Some people are adrenalin junkies and love the high they get from the risk they take in gambling, but not me.

Ever sat in the front row of a comedy show? If you buy a front row seat at any comedy skit then you had better be prepared for not just the jokes the comedian is about to make, but to also be picked on, made fun of, or to be part of the comedian's show.

Comedians are quick witted, observant, and relatable. They look for the 'funny' in situations and are able to bring the situation to life by painting a picture that is easy to follow and leads up to an ending that leaves people laughing in their seats. How many times have you seen the comedian call out to someone in the audience and asks a question or makes some generic observation that gets the audience laughing?

Ever seen that one guy that gets called out in the front row and then gets really defensive over the joke?

The comedian notices two people sitting together and he starts picking on the couple and goes on and on about how the man must have oodles of money because the woman definitely didn't pick him for his good looks. The comedian then starts to dig in and insinuates how rich the man in this couple is because not only is he not as good looking, but he has an accent, his shirt looks like his mom picked it out and he's from some area of the globe that can't usually afford the price of a comedy ticket.

The man gets upset and starts yelling back. He feels the need to protect his heritage and defend the idea that the beautiful woman he is with is not with him only for his money. Although the audience is laughing, this guy is not. He came to watch the comedian make fun of other people, not himself. In the end, he grabs his girlfriend's hand and they walk out.

If you are going to go to a comedy show you know that the sole purpose is to make people laugh. This is done through stereotyping, self-deprecating, finding the humor in any situation. You also know that if you sit in the front of the room that you are more likely to be called on than if you're sitting in the back. No comedian is going to call on someone sitting in the back row, it's entirely too hard to communicate and they probably can't see that far back.

If you make the decision to go to a comedy show, especially if you sit in the front row, then you had better be armed with strong emotional boundaries. Even if you aren't called on, you may be part of the stereotype of the joke. Do you have a bald head, are you short, are you tall, are you fat, are you skinny, are you young, are you old? Doesn't matter what you are-you may have a joke made about something that relates to you. You can't blame the comedian for making a joke at your expense, it's comedy, it's expected. If you don't want to get made fun of, then just like me with gambling, maybe it's best to just stay home.

Strong emotional boundaries will keep you on an even keel and less likely to have an explosive response. If you find you are at peace, then likely you have been able to set the right emotional boundaries in place for the given situation. If you fly off the handle easily, then get inside your head and see where you need to dial into your emotional side and retune the sensitivity level.

Both emotional and intellectual boundaries help you get in tune with the appropriate response in different situations. You become more harmonious with what is happening around you and you can protect yourself when you realize when these situations are occurring.

Paying attention to the people you are talking to, how you are talking to them, what you are saying, or if you allow emotions to drive your actions are all things to help guide you to strengthening your response in these areas. Strong emotional and intellectual boundaries are characteristics of a strong and respectable leader. Aim to know your limits, understand your boundaries, and strive to not disrupt the universe in an adverse way.

Chapter 11: Spiritual Boundaries- A Macro Perspective

Ever wanted something so badly but didn't get it? Ever find that maybe what you wanted really wasn't what you wanted after all?

Ever been laid off from a job, only to find something much better?

Have you ever had a failed relationship with someone you thought you were going to marry, only to find that person wasn't really the love of your life, but in fact your now spouse is?

Remember when you took that exam 3 times to get that job, but then you realized that the job or the life that would have gone with the job were not what you wanted?

Do you remember when you were stuck inside when that pandemic swept the globe and you thought the world was going to end? You panicked, you got depressed, your anxiety was through the roof, but then you started to adjust. Do you remember how it ended up being a blessing because you got to reconnect with your spouse, you enhanced your relationship with your children, you even dug deep and reconnected with yourself?

Sometimes there is something happening in the world at a macro level that we cannot see, but it exists. What we want right in front of us make sense to us in our own minds, but the universe has something else in mind, which ends up being better.

Have you ever thought that maybe the universe has someone or something omnipotent that is a over your life and in control? Something that can see 10 steps ahead of you and can help you navigate? Maybe you see a job loss, but it's actually opening up a door that you were supposed to walk through.

How much peace would you have in knowing that all decisions in the world didn't rest on your shoulders and that you really could never be wrong? You're the one with the freedom to make the moves, but the answers were all found with this omnipotent higher power if you just asked and listened. Failures were not failures, they were lessons or course corrections.

When I made the decision to turn my life over to my higher power, God in my case, my view of the world completely shifted. For years, I was putting all of the emphasis and the responsibility on me to do everything. What I learned was that on my own, I can steer my ship into the ground. Even with a higher power in my life my end result might look different than what I anticipated, but they're no longer failures.

There's something bigger at hand

I wanted so badly to get into the Department of State. The idea of living in countries around the globe for 2-year stints excited me. I had already been around the world, and the thought of doing that for a full-time job was an idea I welcomed. I even contracted with the Department of State, worked down in the Main State building on 23rd Street in Washington, D.C. and at the U.S. Embassy in Kabul, Afghanistan. I knew this was what I wanted, I loved everything about the life it promised.

I took the exam for the first time in 2009. I had just completed my MBA program, I was married with a husband that was excited for the prospect of living abroad, and I was fired up. Test results came back and I wasn't accepted into the program.

No problem, I'll just try again. In 2010, I tried again. Got the test results back and I wasn't accepted.

No problem, I'll just try again. In 2012, I tried again. Got the test results back and I wasn't accepted.

I certainly could have kept going, but what I didn't realize was this was a 'Jen decision' that wasn't part of my divine plan.

Looking back now, I'm grateful I wasn't accepted. Although it's a necessary job and I have the highest respect for those that are accepted and represent this great nation, it's not a life I believe I would have ultimately wanted, nor do I believe it was an occupation where I could have had my maximum impact on the world. I found that I rather like being in my home for a duration of time, I love the simple life I live in Dallas, Texas, and I find satisfaction in helping to impact and transform lives.

Sure, it seemed disappointing at the time to take a test and never pass it, but I never consulted with my God to see if that was even the direction I should have been heading. I headed where I wanted to and didn't take advantage of the free advice.

Having a higher power with a macro perspective of the world is like being connected to the director of a movie who knows the ending. When a situation arises I know there's an ending, and I know it's a good ending. His promise includes "plans to prosper you and not to harm you, to give you a hope and a future" Jeremiah 29:11.

When I need help, I know it's nothing my God can't handle. When I need advice, I know my God will be there. When it seems I 'fail', I know my God will be there. When I start veering in the wrong direction, I know my God will be there to get me back on track. This doesn't always mean that my life will be a cake

walk with roses, but I know He will be there and I
know sometimes I need to be taught lessons or brought
back on course.

I've come to accept this power greater than myself and
it's the most powerful force I could have around me.
Couple this force with boundaries and you've become a
powerhouse. One that has peace, a guide, someone
that is looking out for you, someone that always has
your best interest in mind, one that you can let go and
let God. Let God do His good works, let God bear the
burden, let God handle the situation. He already
knows the ending so ask advise and accept the course
corrections along the way.

By the time I was 30, I had failed the Department of
State exam 3 times, I had changed job tracks at least 3
times, I was battling with addiction and all my lows
that came with that, I was divorced- I was being taught
lessons and being course corrected across every area of
my life.

Accepting that there is something much bigger at hand
is like being handed a gift. If you move in a direction
that doesn't come to fruition then it's not a failure.
Sure, it can be disappointing, but if you are in the
mindset that it's because there is something better for
you, that there's a brighter path you need to journey
on, that there's a different ending that has peace and
hope- then it turns course corrections into grace, into
favor, into kindness.

Have Faith

Faith is the "confidence in what we hope for and assurance about what we do not see" Hebrews 11:1. It gives us courage, it provides stability, and it gives us strength.

When you know that you are going to be ok, should you worry?

If you know you have the most powerful force behind you, should you be more confident?

If you believe you have the assurance of peace and hope, should you question if you 'seemingly fail' or should you trust that you're being guided towards that peace and hope?

Faith is believing and to trust God even when we don't understand. If you step out in faith and allow God to work through you then you will be able to accomplish things you may never know you were capable of.

On August 5th, 2010, 33 miners were trapped in a Chilean mining accident. This copper and gold mine opened back in 1889, and more than a century later it now had 33 hard-working men trapped inside with minimal rations to eat and drink.

The world fixated around the mine and the lives of those trapped inside, it became global news. Families and friends waited as crews tried to dig these men out, only to be greeted with another land spill on August 7th.

 It wasn't until August 22 that drills and cameras were able to make their way to the men and remarkably they found all 33 men to be alive and well. Families rejoiced as they found out about the news of their loved ones, but they weren't out of the woods yet. Through this small hole the men were given food and water, and for another month and a half this was their life.

On October 13, 2010, an astounding 69 days after the collapse, all 33 men walked out of the mine. It was a miracle that was shared around the world. People united with cheers and love for the families that had just been reunited (6).

Mario Sepulveda, one of the miners, greeted friends and family and issued this encouraging message "we always knew that we would be rescued, we never lost faith (7)."

Faith can get us through the hardest of times if we just believe there is something better that is around the corner, that there is something to look forward to, that there is peace and not evil to give you a future and hope.

If you allow faith into your life and allow it to grow you, then you'll get through things you never would

have imagined. For Mario and the 32 other men, I
don't imagine any of them foresaw the events that
occurred on August 5th. Their faith remained strong
and all 33 came out on the other end embracing their
families with hugs and smiles.

Your higher power can make all things possible, if you
believe, if you have faith.

Faith trumps fear

How do you know how deep your faith is, and how
can you tell how strong your spiritual boundaries and
beliefs lay? One question:

Do you have fear?

If you have fear, then you need to dial up your faith.
Your higher power has control over the situation, so
why do you fear? Those miners believed that even as
they were enclosed by the earth that they were going to
come out of that mine alive. 69 days, over 2 months
later, the miners prevailed with their faith it
superseded their fear. All 33 men walked out alive,
nothing short of a modern may miracle.

If there is a promise of a good future with peace then
why fear? Again, fear does not produce results, it's a
response- it does not produce outcomes.

It's free consultative advice

Ever needed to use a lawyer? Even if you spent 10 minutes on the phone you still got a bill for at minimum $100. When a trial goes to court you could end up spending thousands upon thousands of dollars, and it seems sometimes the only one that wins in a case is the lawyer because of all the hefty court costs and legal fees.

Imagine you had the direct line to the person that had all the answers, knew the players, knew the ending. Imagine that cost, but for you it's entirely free- all you need to do is ask. That's pretty incredible if you ask me.

Your higher power wants a relationship with you, wants to talk with you, wants to give you peace and hope. In an expensive world, there's not much that comes truly free. This is an unending relationship and your higher power will always be there- even if you veer.

When you know you have the most powerful force in the Universe behind you, when you have access to advice from the Omnipotent, when you and let go and let your higher power handle the situation- imagine the position that puts you in? There is an entire book written that gives guidance for how people should live, so if we don't follow it are we just reinventing the wheel? For thousands of years the Bible has guided people.

Prominent figures we have come to now as household names have claimed a higher power over their lives:

- Alice Cooper
- George Foreman
- Jane Fonda
- Justin Furstenfeld
- Martin Luther King
- C.S. Lewis
- Thomas Edison
- Rosa Parks
- Wolfgang Amadeus Mozart
- Sir Isaac Newton
- Susan B. Anthony
- Charles Dickens

These folks don't claim perfection, and some came to know their higher power after realizing the chaos and dysfunction their life had when they walked alone (8).

I have the freedom to make decisions, to live my life, to do things my way, and I have faith that I have someone with a much larger picture looking out for me and guiding my path. I know I make mistakes, I don't always seemingly succeed in what I'm doing, but I learn and I course correct.

I have a sense of tranquility about my life knowing that

the end result is to live a prosperous life, one full of peace. When I was laid-off I knew it wasn't my time, but it was God's time. It was time for me to go full steam ahead in the direction I had been praying for, where I could be of maximum impact to the world. When the pandemic swept over the globe I didn't panic or get anxious, I knew there was something much larger happening and I had faith we were going to make it through.

What were some of those positives and might that bigger picture be? I won't claim to know the answer (and maybe there's more than one), but I'll state some observations of good that came from the pandemic.

- People that had financial stability stepped in to help those who were less fortunate
- The entire world shared one common goal
- The government stepped in and offered immediate support
- Pollution levels dropped
- Families got to reacquaint with one another
- People had a greater appreciation for the feeling of hug
- Many people drew closer to their higher-power and found solace
- The world learned how to better prepare for such a global event
- People with hectic schedules got to take a breath
- We got to reassess our priorities
- We learned to be more self-sufficient

- We learned how to work from home
- Many experienced a better work/life balance
- People became innovative in how to grow their business

I don't know the master plan or the *why* behind the pandemic, but I do know that if we focus our mind on the good, if we look at it opportunistically, if we trust there's a larger picture at hand, if we know that the ultimate state is peace and not of harm- then we should be able to reduce, if not eliminate, anxiety and fear.

Let it go, stop trying to control the things that are out of your control and give that to the Master of the Universe, the Almighty, the Higher Power that governs all. It's not on you, and remember, stress and anxiety does not equal results.

How does spirituality and boundaries overlap? First, if you've made the decision to let go, then that is a standard you have in your life. When situations arise then you immediately arm yourself with spiritual beliefs that create boundaries to protect you from negativity.

Do you have boundaries around your relationship or how you connect with the spiritual side throughout your life? Maybe you structure your mornings to include a quiet time, or maybe you hit your knees before you go to bed to have that conversation with your higher power.

I know when I didn't have any boundaries around communication with my higher power that it almost never existed. When I wasn't concerned with having my higher power as a priority, it never became one. I had to create a habit in my life to start that communication and that dialogue.

You may also decide that you do not wish to engage in or hear certain words that are considered foul. You may choose not to curse or listen to anything that includes cursing. You may decide that you are not willing to go to an R Rated movie or listen to music that claims to have Explicit language. These are boundaries you put around what you listen to that are against your beliefs (spiritual or not).

Whatever is going to connect you or disconnect you from your relationship with your Master of the Universe is a spiritual boundary.

Center your life around a higher power and let go of the weight and the pressure you put on yourself to drive your ship. Create the structure that breeds constant communication. No relationship will work well if it's sporadic. It's peace, it's comfort, it's hope, it's faith, it's power.

Now, couple these spiritual beliefs and boundaries with mental boundaries and watch your mindset be so rock solid and shielded from external forces that not even an event as uneasy and terrifying as a pandemic will shake you.

Chapter 12: Armed by Mental Boundaries

Mental boundaries, in my opinion, is that protective layer around you. They can be used independently or coupled with other boundaries. Those mental boundaries, your mindset, is your perspective, and your perspective is your reality. You have the ability to block anything and to create any reality you choose. This is where the rubber meets the road and is your defense to anything that comes into your mental path. Your mind is the most powerful asset you have, if you know how to use it.

Mental boundaries are like a shield, they protect what you don't want from entering the brain. This is your view on the world. How can someone see the good in things when everything is seemingly falling apart? It's because they have mental boundaries that block the negativity from entering their mind. Your mental boundaries will make you indestructible and untouchable.

In 2020, one of the most powerful vehicles ever put on the road came into production. The Hennessey Venom F5 engine produces 1817 horsepower and 1193 lb-ft of torque. If you're not familiar with the Venom F5, let's put it in perspective (9).

Ferrari is one of the more well-known fast and exotic cars. This Italian brand is known for the high-end and high-price tag of their vehicles. They not only limit the number of vehicles they produce, but they also are exclusive to whom they'll sell their vehicles. If you win the lottery, that doesn't necessarily give you the right to buy certain Ferraris. In fact, some of their models are so exclusive that there is a requirement that you must have owned a certain number of Ferrari vehicles before being considered to own one of them. Ferrari, like many of the high-end manufactures, does this so they maintain a certain status and exclusivity. The engine in the 2020 Ferrari Roma produces 612 horsepower and 560 lb-ft of torque. It claims the car can go from 0-62 mph in 3.4 seconds and is one sexy vehicle, but costs over $225,000 USD (10).

Probably more familiar in mainstream American society is a Nissan Maxima. Anyone is not only eligible to buy one, but they are mass produced and readily available at a reasonable price. The engine produces 300 horsepower and 261 lb-ft of torque. This mainstream vehicle goes from 0-60 mph in 5.9 seconds, and hits maximum speeds of 160 mph. It's average cost will set you back $35k USD (11). Now, let's go back to that Hennessey.

With that as the baseline, the Hennessey Venom F5 will go from 0-60 mph in less than 2 seconds and can reach speeds up to 300 mph. For the time it takes some people to stand up, this majestic vehicle can be cruising at 60 mph. If eligible to buy, this luxury vehicle will cost you $1.6M for the base vehicle, with the option to scale up from there. For $2M you can have one of the world's most powerful luxury street vehicles (9).

Imagine you have a Hennessey sitting in your garage and you're not aware how fast it can go or the cost. You're headed to the grocery store and you decide to drive this striking and unique looking vehicle. Not ever having driven one, you drive the vehicle just like would your Nissan Maxima. As you pull out of your driveway you start noticing people pointing and staring in your direction. As you stop at the stoplights you have vehicles pull up next to you, rev their engines, and speed away as the light turns green.

Little do you know that you are sitting in one of the world's fastest and most expensive vehicles and if you wanted to race these common street cars that you would easily blow them away. You also get to benefit from the luxuries, quality and performance of the vehicle, the prestige that goes along with owning one, and the investment potential which is much higher than any run of the mill vehicle. You may even have opportunity to attend certain events that you might not otherwise be able to attend.

Now imagine you are a Hennessey and yet you treat your life like a Maxima. Are you getting what you paid for? Are you taking advantage of the speed, the features, the power, the opportunities, or are you merely using your Hennessey for driving to the store for milk?

Your mind is a Venom F5. You are not a Maxima, but if you're not using your mind in the way it was designed for, then you are wasting thousands of thousands, if not millions of opportunities to reach your full potential.

How do you know what kind of vehicle you are?

Simple.

You're the Venom F5. You have the potential to scale to be a $2M vehicle that goes from 0-60 in less than 2 seconds and has 1817 horsepower and 1193 lb-ft of torque, you are built to be a machine.

Mental boundaries are how you get to be that machine. They'll make you stronger, faster and more agile than any of your competition. We're talking about your thought process that leads you to your thoughts, opinions, perception, your reality. Your mind can shield you from anything, which makes you stronger than your opponent.

Imagine you trained your mind to always look at the positive aspect of a situation. Imagine that even when that pandemic swept the earth that instead of panicking you:

- Spent more time with your family
- Picked up a project you've been putting to the side
- Studied the market and came up with a new marketing strategy and business model for your business
- Found ways to give back to the community
- Reconnected with your spouse
- Reconnected with yourself
- Bonded closer with your higher power
- Finally treated yourself to a 'you night'
- Cooked a special meal to show your family how much you appreciated them
- Networked with others to talk about new business opportunities
- Wrote a book

And what if when you got laid off you:
- Cut back on unnecessary spending and brought it down to the basics
- Applied for unemployment, if applicable
- Talked to your spouse about that million-dollar idea you've been dreaming about for years and finally went for it
- Came to the conclusion that it may not have been your timing, but you knew there was something much more divine and bigger at play and you being laid off was the sign you needed from your higher power to take a different path
- You chose not to panic and told yourself it was going to be ok

Mental boundaries are everything, they are your most powerful weapon against the world. When I got laid off and the coronavirus hit my mind stayed positive and I focused on what I could control and had faith it was the right move.

If you want to go into a state of paralysis with fear and paranoia, then that is a choice you can make. It's those mental boundaries that lead you to the proper state of mind and perspective on life.

I've heard this over and over, 'but Jen, I have to stress, I have young kids.' 'but Jen, I have to stress, I have a mortgage.' No, you need to follow through with your responsibilities, and that has nothing to do with if you are stressed or at peace. *Being in a state of panic, fear, anxiety or stress does not equal results.* You make the decision on your state of mind. Period, end of story. The world is going to continue to move regardless of how you set your mind or react to what is going on around you.

What about death? What about when someone comes up behind you and scares you? What if you get a diagnosis from the doctor and you're given 2 months to live?

These are all legitimate feelings and I don't want to minimize your naturally human response. You might feel fear, sadness or confusion. These are all tough things to go through, and as humans it's a normal response to feel. But, even in those dark times we still have options. It may take us to get through the initial shock of the news, but you have the power to make any of these situations positive. Your mind will shape your perception.

Death is tough, but maybe you find peace in knowing the person went to Heaven. Or maybe there is peace in knowing the person is no longer suffering. Or maybe you find peace in knowing the person had a positive impact on others. You have the choice to look favorably at the situation and remember the good moments. Although your heart hurts, you push yourself into that happy space and make the choice to stay that way. It's ok to grieve, as we discussed, allow yourself that. I want you to still find the good and the positive and don't get stuck in the past.

That is power!

The mental boundaries you put in place have everything to do with your perception, and your perception is reality!

Is it that simple? YES!

I spent years of my life in a negative state of mind, and I think it's easy for all of us to do. You turn on the news and the world seems to be falling apart. It's easy to get caught up in the whirlwind, but you don't have to. Set your standards to happiness, look for the opportunity, look for the positivity, and then when situations arise use those boundaries to keep you from going in the gutter.

- I was laid off- I had the opportunity to focus on my business full-time
- I was laid off- I eliminated unnecessary spending
- I was laid off- I got to write my next book
- I was laid off- I had time to focus on marketing my book, "RESET", which launched as an Amazon #1 Best Seller
- I was laid off- I finally started getting 8 hours of sleep everyday (not just the weekend)
- I was laid off- I was finally out of a toxic work environment and redirected my energies full-time where I could be of maximum service to my God to help others

You always have choices, and you've giving up your power if you think otherwise. You can armor your mind with boundaries to keep yourself in a positive space and you'll be amazed at how positive your world becomes.

You may need to come up with a justification in your mind to help you get to that space, I do that all the time- especially when I'm on the road. When I see a driver that is completely erratic it can be frustrating. Sometimes I have to tell myself that the person driving must have an emergency or a baby on the way, which helps me calm my instinct instead of focusing on the driving (which, is not something I control anyway).

People used to offend me all the time when they would talk about my height. Little comments that may have been entirely harmless I would translate as negative and I would internalize them. Then one day, I decided to finally accept my height and I chose to block any negative comments or interpret all comments and intentions for the good. Now, if someone says something that could be translated as mean, or even if it is outright mean, like a shield- I block it. Not entering here! I love me, I love all of me, you don't steal my joy- end of story.

You will not steal my joy!

I have an internal dialogue in my head when a situation arises that seemingly could be interpreted negatively and I say 'you will not steal my joy!'

In my corporate career, I had a boss who was wildly offensive and delivered his message through his joking demeanor. He was direct and to the point, and there was nothing subtle when he spoke. He was known for his aggressive approach in the office, and he crossed the line of mentoring and leadership and came across as an offensive jerk. His team and colleagues would talk about their lack of respect for him because his leadership title didn't align with his 'leadership qualities' (or lack thereof). It was almost like watching a Saturday Night Live clip where Chris Farley was the main character. The only difference was there was an underlying knifing that was happening. There was always some element of comedy and humor in his words and delivery, but each time he would publicly roast anyone that he felt needed to 'do better'. Without fail, every meeting would be like watching one of those shows on Comedy Central where the audience is amused at one person's expense, and you just hoped it wouldn't be your turn.

Now, I don't believe this boss of mine was cognizant of just how offensive he was being. I certainly believe in constructive criticism, building up skills and working as a team to problem solve, but there are more effective ways of communicating. Belittling someone and making them feel like they're 2 inches tall in front of their coworkers is not, in my opinion, the right approach. You might drive people to get the results you want, but was it done in the most respectable and 'leadership-like' way?

How do you navigate this situation when you feel like you are sitting in the hot seat and being publicly persecuted? First, you have basic rights that we'll talk about in the next chapter. You have the right to walk away, you have the right to stand up for yourself, you have the right to say no. This doesn't mean you have to stoop down to his level and play dirty. You can do so in a very professional manner. Consider the source. Secondly, arm yourself with strong mental boundaries.

When these situations happen tell yourself immediately that 'it will not steal my joy'. Say this over and over. Whenever there is something that seemingly would get you down, something that causes pain or anxiety, anything that rubs you the wrong way then commit to yourself that you not let it take your joy, because that too is your right.

- You get laid off- 'it will not steal my joy'
- A friendship ends- 'it will not steal my joy'
- An unexpected bill comes- 'it will not steal my joy'
- Your boss is a jerk- 'it will not steal my joy'
- Your kid says something you know they don't mean (or maybe they do)- 'it will not steal my joy'
- Your spouse wants a divorce- 'it will not steal my joy'

I hold tight onto that statement, it has become my mantra. When I keep myself in that mindset then, like a shield, I am keeping out the unwanted feelings.

Let what you can and cannot control be your guide and focus on those areas. Tune your mind to optimism and positivity and watch your life start to transform. Do not let anything steal your joy, block it when it comes flying at you.

You are driving a Nissan Maxima if you are in anything but a positive state of mind. Get out of your average vehicle and go grab the keys to your Venom F5. You are the most powerful person on the road, go shield all the unwanted thoughts and negativity from entering your mind. Remember, negativity won't yield you results, so you don't *have to* live in fear and be anxious, that's your choice- activate your mental boundaries and let go.

Mental boundaries, that's power, and you want to be driving that Hennessey. It's free and accessible to you. But what if I told you that yes, it's power, but coupling it with that macro perspective will take your life, your mind, your entire experience on this earth to its maximum potential! Know your vehicle, the features and how to use them. Tune the radio to happiness and positivity. Practice them until they becomes natural. It may take time, but trust me- you learned negativity, you can also unlearn it.

Chapter 13: Understanding your basic rights

When establishing your boundaries, it's essential you understand your basic rights as a human.

The government, for example, gives you certain fundamental rights as a citizen (talking US specifically here). These include the right to vote, the freedom of religion, freedom of speech, freedom of the press, the right to bear arms, the right against unreasonable searches and seizures, the right to life, liberty and the pursuit of happiness. The United States Constitution clearly spells out the governing rights to which citizens are entitled to.

If the government is going to explicitly lay out the rights of citizens for governance purposes, shouldn't you understand your own basic rights so you can govern your life?

Imagine if a police officer walked up to you one day and arrested you. No words were uttered, you were simply put in handcuffs. There was no reason, justification, or explanation from the officer. You were just shackled and thrown in the back of a cop car and taken to jail.

Regardless if you had done something or not, it is your

basic right to know and understand the rights to which you are entitled in that situation. In the 1966 U.S. Supreme Court case, Miranda v Arizona, the court mandated that all persons being placed under arrest must be read their rights.

> "You have the right to remain silent. Anything you say can be used against you in court. You have the right to talk to a lawyer for advice before we ask you any questions. You have the right to have a lawyer with you during questioning. If you cannot afford a lawyer, one will be appointed for you before any questioning if you wish. If you decide to answer questions now without a lawyer present, you have the right to stop answering at any time (12)."

Imagine that same police officer opening your front door and walking through your house without permission. What you should ask for is a warrant, because a search warrant must be in place if the officer is looking for evidence.

These are your basic rights, and you hold authority to those rights. You know that if you are not read your Miranda Rights when being arrested, if there's no search warrant when your house is searched, then legally you have a case that can be taken to the court of law.

The same holds true to how you need to view your

own rights, and you need to hold yourself to those rights.

You have the right to say NO

You have the right to say NO. At any time, in any situation, you always have options. It is within your right to tell someone, or a group, or yourself NO!

Saying NO can be incredibly difficult, especially if you're a people pleaser. If you are always trying to make everyone happy, then it's likely you have a difficult time saying NO. If you practice it or not, it's a fundamental right you have as a human to say and to practice. It establishes clarity in boundaries. If you outright say NO then you've made your position clear on where you stand.

It's not only your right, but it's a building block, a tool and a way to liberate yourself from having unwanted people, places, things and ideologies in your space.

Saying NO actually gives you back power over your life. Two simple letters can communicate such a strong message. If someone asks you to do something you don't want to, say NO. Simple as that. It communicates to them where you stand on an issue. That's your boundary, and that's power.

I look back at my own life and where I needed to learn to say NO. I worked for a company and I gave them everything I had: time, sanity, they even chose my zip code. I was willing to go way above and beyond, I said yes to everything. I never could get out of a state of chaos, I was constantly giving more and more, and I felt like I was drinking from a fire hose every day. I didn't want that level of stress and anxiety in my life, but I never pushed back otherwise. What I communicated to the company was that I was ok with the amount of work I was doing, and they gave me exactly what I was willing to accept. I watched people around me that had families and relationships that would go home at the end of the day not stressed and crazed, yet I was constantly in a state of frenzy. I had no one to blame other than myself. It wasn't the company that crossed the boundary, it was me not saying NO when I needed to.

It's not just telling others NO, it's also telling yourself so that you get to say YES to you in the end. It's your given right. Practice it and hold true to yourself.

You have the right to put yourself first

You have the right to put yourself first. You might want to read that again. It's not selfish, it's your right.

What I learned having gone through my own transformation, was that I could give more of me when I was taking care of myself. Ever flown on a plane? What do they tell you? In the event of an emergency, put your mask on before assisting others. If you don't put your oxygen and lifeline on first, then you will run out of breath and not be effective to anyone. In your life this might come in the form of a breakdown, depression, anxiety, sickness, or put you into a state of panic when all you needed to do was put yourself first.

When I focused on my self-care, when I spent time self-reflecting, and when I put me first then I was better able to assist others with their masks. If I was conserving air or blue in the face from not breathing, then I didn't have the energy, the will, the ability to help others. It's not selfish, it's your right.

In addition to myself, I've seen disastrous results when people neglect their own wellbeing. A client of mine called me when life was seemingly hitting a rock-bottom. As I listened to him talk I didn't hear of anything he was doing for himself. He was a good husband, father, he had to take care of his father when he was ill, he put food on the table for his family and a roof over their heads, he volunteered at his son's school, and he was active in the community. On paper, this man had an impressive resume of things he was doing. What I didn't hear was that he was doing anything for himself. I asked him when he took time for himself and he brushed off the question. I could see there was immense guilt this man had around even thinking about doing anything for himself. The problem was that he had become disconnected from the person within and life was piling on him unknowingly.

Here he was, this great man that had accomplished so many things and yet he felt he was about to snap. Why? In part, he didn't put himself first. There's only so much we can take when we don't take care of the person that is taking care of everyone else. After working together, what he found was that he could still accomplish everything he did before *and* put himself first. In fact, he found that he was more joyous in helping others because he was feeding his own soul.

You have the right to walk away

You have the right to walk away. No one can force you into anything you don't want to be forced into.

Ever seen a bull rider on a bull? Their goal is to stay on for 8 seconds. If they can ride that bull for all 8 seconds, then they've accomplished what they set out for. But how many of them actually make it? Bulls are fierce, they're strong, and they don't want to be sat upon and rode. The males typically weigh over 2,000 pounds. That's solid mass that gets launched into a stadium with a comparably tiny human on its back. Not anything I am personally interested in.

Ever seen a rider get launched off the back of the kicking bull? What does he do?

He runs.

That bull is out for revenge, and it's in the best interest for the crew to calm that bull and get it back in its pen. If the rider chooses to stay put, to not get out of reach from the bull, that might be the last ride he ever takes.

You have the right to walk away. You might not physically have a bull coming at you, but you might metaphorically speaking, and you had better move if you don't want to get hurt or if you simply don't want to be involved in the situation.

You have the right to communicate

Just like the constitution, you have the right to communicate. It is your inherent right to let others know how to treat you, if they've crossed a line, or to let them know how you feel. If this is done by walking away, saying no, or through other verbal or non-verbal modes of communication- it's your given right.

We'll talk through this in the next chapter, but ingrain it in your mind that it's a right you need to exercise, and is a key component when we start to structure our lives.

You have the right to be treated with respect

You have the right to be treated with respect. It's a

choice, and you own it. When you were born, God didn't give you the short end of the stick and tell you that you lost your right to be respected. We all have the right to be respected, and if you are not then tap into your rights and boundaries for your next steps (walk away, politely say something, interpret what is being said as a positive instead of a negative).

If only I understood this when I was growing up. Imagine being 6 feet tall at 14 years old (184cm), oh, and a female.

"Hey, how's the air up there?"

"It's the jolly green giant!"

"Why do you wear heels? You don't need to be any taller!"

"You're very feminine. Most tall girls look like drag queens!"

If I only understood what boundaries were, I may have heard all of those phrases differently and responded in a way that would have protected my heart. To be clear, I interpreted them all negatively. I didn't give myself the respect I deserved to kindly tell anyone that those comments hurt me. You don't always have to tell people when you don't feel respected, you can just block it from entering your brain, but I didn't have that boundary laid out in my head. I still hear comparable comments about my height today, but I've learned to just block any negative thoughts around them, I don't pay them any mind, and I move on with my happy life. Not only did I allow people to disrespect me, but even more so, I disrespected myself by not having those boundaries in place.

You have the right to feel however you want!

You have the right to feel however you want! You choose if you want to be happy, sad, mad, anxious, or even just OK. You have that right to choose, no one is making you do otherwise. My advice would be to stay in a happy, peaceful, joyous state, but you certainly could choose to live with anxiety, panic, fear or worry if you wanted.

It's entirely your call. It's important to understand what your objective is for yourself as you start to assess your boundaries, so that you can make sure you set them up properly.

Personally, I choose happy.

I mentioned the comments I get about my height, some of them are no different today when I choose happiness than when I had no boundaries around these comments and I interpreted them all negatively. "Why do you wear heels, you're tall enough"

Let's dissect that.

When I had no boundaries and no decision made on how I chose to feel:

- I heard in my head: you're too tall, you're not normal, sexy shoes aren't made for someone of your size, you should try to be as short as you can, you must be some kind of freak.
- How did I feel: depressed, sad, lonely, angry

Now, with boundaries and me choosing happiness

- I hear in my head: OK! Poor souls don't realize they sound ignorant. Wonder if they're insecure. They might just be jealous. Just wait until you need me to reach something on the top shelf for you, I'll still reach it for ya!
- How do I feel: Great! I don't have any emotions tied to that comment because I took away its power.

It's not only happy or sad that you can feel, you don't have to be either a jolly feller or a negative Nancy, it's also OK to just be OK. If you've looked on social media, it's easy to believe that everyone has a picture-perfect life. No one posts on the dysfunction or what people don't want you to see. People post rainbows and kitty cats, vacations and happiness. We're led to believe that people have these beautiful lives, peaceful, happy, successful, and rarely will you see the other side of the coin. It gives the impression that our lives always need to look like they do on Instagram and Facebook. In case you hadn't figured it out, that's not always reality!

My life did not look like Instagram or Facebook. My life was not OK. Even in the throes of my internal battles, I still managed to post pictures portraying happiness. It's usually a façade. Many people do it (I'll tell you now that I believe my social media matches my life!).

Regardless of what social media shows, you need to know it's your right to just be OK.

As we mentioned before, but I want you to really understand the importance, life can present itself with challenges and many of them can conjure up emotions. Experiencing the death of a loved one, a troubling diagnosis from the doctor, or going through a trauma can all bring about intense feelings. Just because you establish boundaries in your life does not mean you fail if you're feeling sad or just OK about things. Take the time to grieve, just make sure you are working towards bringing yourself to a state of happiness again. I believe these are opportunities to assess what is happening and connect deeper with ourselves.

When I was going through these especially rough times

where I was just feeling OK, I set a goal on getting to a better place, and worked to get there.

It's OK just to be OK, but work towards that happy place if that's where you want to be.
You have the right to feel how you want, you're in control of that choice.

Knowing your rights give you power. If you didn't know you had the right to say NO, if you didn't know you had the right to be happy, if you didn't know you had the right to put yourself first, if you didn't know you had the right to be treated with respect, if you didn't know you had the right to walk away then would you?

Knowing your rights will give light to not only how others should treat you, but also how you should treat yourself. They provide guidelines on when to make a move, what your limits are, and how you should respond.

If you know your Constitutional Rights, if you know the police can't come into your home without a warrant, if you know you need to be read your Miranda Rights before being arrested, then you should also know your personal rights as a human being and hold yourself to them.

Do not feel conflicted about establishing boundaries

using these rights. If you are a people-pleaser it might feel awkward to say NO, but, it's your right so you need to feel comfortable upholding and adhering to all the basic rights you've been given. If you don't, then other's probably won't either. You can say NO, you can walk away, you can put yourself first, and at some point you might need to do all of those things. You might not be the most popular person, but you'll have respect, you'll have self-respect as well. If someone isn't willing to respect you and your rights then do you need that person in your life? Read this chapter again and really get a feel for understanding and exercising your basic rights- they belong to you, but they only hold value if you uphold them.

Chapter 14: In tune with your feelings

Remember when you were back in kindergarten and there was the poster on the wall that had 200 different 'smiley faces' with different moods? Your teacher would have you point out which one you were feeling and share it with the class. You would look at the faces, think about your mood and think about all the things that happened that day.

- Do I feel EXHAUSTED?
  - No, I took a nap during nap time.
- Do I feel HAPPY?
  - Yes! I made a beautiful picture during art class that I'm going to give my daddy for his birthday.
- Do I feel DISGUSTED?
  - A little bit. Johnny squished a worm and I didn't like it.
- Do I feel GUILTY?
  - I did feel a little guilty when I stole my friend's eraser and kept it.
- Do I feel EMBARRASSED?
  - A little. I farted and turned red.
- Do I feel LONELY?
  - No, my friends are all here.

You'd go down the list of 200 faces, until you landed on

one. The one that describes your general mood, and you probably chose happy, sad or angry.

The truth is, there are tons of feelings.

- Frightened
- Mischievous
- Confident
- Overwhelmed
- Cautious
- Jealous
- Hysterical
- Anxious
- Paranoid
- Ecstatic
- Suspicious
- Smug
- Depressed
- Hopeful
- Lovestruck
- Ashamed

These are not all 'child feelings', but life does tend to have more complex feelings as we get older. But as adults, no one is forcing us to look at a poster of feelings and pick which one we associate with and figure out why. Yet all of them help us to understand where we are emotionally, and where we want to be. Knowing where we want to be will then help us to identify the boundaries we want to put in our lives.

If you are experiencing hysteria, what is causing that? What do you need to eliminate or do differently in your life so you don't feel that emotion? How do we then take where you are and get you to a state of happiness or peace? Baselining where you are at will help you identify what needs to be worked on to get you where you want to be.

Those same children are encouraged not just to put an emotion on the paper, but to also talk about the why.

"Little Tommy, why did you say you are sad today?"

"Because my friend drew on my paper."

"Tommy, why does that make you sad?"

"Because I wanted to draw on this paper and give it to my dad."

"Angie, why did you say you are excited today?"

"Because my mom made me pancakes this morning!"

"Angie, why does that make you excited?"

"Because pancakes are delicious and they're my favorite!"

These conversations are about as rudimentary as they

come, but they are so powerful. Tommy and Angie both are in tune with their feelings and the both can communicate why they feel that way. Let's look at them a little deeper though.

"Tommy, did you tell your friend you did not want him to draw on your paper?"

"No."

Maybe Tommy could have avoided some angst if he had just communicated the boundaries. Yes, but Jen, what about those people that are going to draw on your paper even if you tell them no? What about those people?

Simple.

If someone doesn't respect the boundaries that you have clearly communicated, then you have the decision on how you address the situation. You may decide that it's not a big deal if someone draws on your paper and it no longer makes you sad. Or, you may decide that if someone cannot respect your boundaries (after you've clearly communicated with them) then do you want to spend time with this person in your life? These are decisions you need to make to keep your boundaries intact. I'm not just referring to a kindergarten class here, I'm talking about in your adult life where you have people that just don't respect your boundaries. If you've communicated them and they get crossed, then you need to decide the next steps on how to handle the situation. Ignoring it, if it truly upsets you, is not effective in addressing your emotions- it just buries them.

"Angie, how did your mom know that pancakes were your favorite?"

"Because I told her, and she makes them for me on special occasions."

Angie's mom knew pancakes made her happy because she told her mom, there was no ambiguity. Angie's mom also had a boundary in place. Instead of giving her pancakes every day, she chose to only do it on special occasions so it was something Angie would look forward to. She communicated this to Angie, and it was a special 'thing' the two could enjoy together.

If Tommy wants to be happy, he cannot live in a world where people are always coloring on his paper.

If Angie wants to be in a happy mood, then she knows that pancakes could do the trick!

They have both learned from their basic life experience what makes them happy or sad. They stopped to assess their feelings and why they felt that way.

It's trial and error throughout life, but we have to be

cognizant of where we are and make decisions based on those feelings. If you don't feel good about yourself when you eat a tub of ice cream in one setting, then you should probably stick to just one bowl. If it makes you angry to think about a past situation, then you should let it go. If you get frustrated trying to play basketball, then don't agree to a game when your friends ask. If you get anxious when you day-trade on the stock market, then stop day-trading.

If you feel good about yourself when you portion your meals, then portion out your meals. If you find enjoyment when you read, then get a library card and go to town. If you get excited when you see tigers, then make it a point to go to the zoo twice a year. If you like the feeling of getting your hair done in a salon, then make it a point to treat yourself and go get your hair done. Even if times are financially tight, you can still find plenty of ways to make yourself feel happy- it doesn't always take money to get there.

It sounds basic because it is. It's what we learned decades ago. But, it's remembering that we have the choice. And, in order to know where we want to be, we have to get in tune with our feelings.

There is no one making life's decisions for you, you need to be in control here. You own the feeling, you own the choice. Once you know where you want to be, then you start to build a life around that goal. For Angie, her mom also put boundaries in place. She wanted to make her daughter happy, but it would be more special and memorable if she made pancakes only on special occasions. It's still a treat, but it's not something that is probably very healthy or reasonable to do every day. Boundaries are healthy and they help level set standards and expectations which allow for more consistent feeling.

What might that look like in your own life?

Let's go back to the example of eliminating panic and anxiety.

What makes you panic? When are you getting those feelings? What is that emotion tied to? Is it what you see on the news? Do you get it from your friends? Are you thinking about the future and what it might entail or not entail? Are you concerned about your retirement? Do you worry your parents may take a fall when you aren't around? Do you worry your child may get wrapped up with the wrong crowd?

Heavy stuff, and legitimate concerns.

You know what makes you panic, now where do you want to be? Let's say, peace. You choose happiness and peace over panic and anxiety.

What in your space, that is within your control, puts you in a peaceful state of mind? How about your happy place? Is there an activity or a state of mind that you can go to when you start to feel anxious?

"Jen, I just got laid off. I have a family to support. How do I stay calm?"

It's your choice.
- Can you apply for unemployment?
- Do you have family that can help out?
- Are there unnecessary expenses you can eliminate for the time being?
- Are you applying for jobs every day and following up?
- Have you looked at temporary job placement services?
- Have you asked your friends if they know anyone is hiring?

I could keep going, but what I hope you grasp is you can sit there and panic and cause an ulcer, or you can start going down your list of what you do control and take action.

First it's that recognition and awareness of your feelings, being in tune with how you are feeling. From there, you can dive into your next steps.

Go find a copy of that smiley-face poster on the internet and look at your options of different feelings. Walk through each one and ask yourself what makes you feel that way. What would need to happen in your life for you to say you're feeling embarrassed, or overwhelmed, or upset, or anxious. What needs to happen in your life for you to feel happiness, peace or a sense of calmness.

Make sure you know what direction you want to head, and if the way you are feeling now does not align with the 'ideal state' then you need to start digging further into your life to assess what is off the rails and where boundaries will help you get to that happy face you desire.

Chapter 15: Communicate

Communication is key to letting others know what boundaries you establish. Every day of your life, you teach people how you want to be treated. Think of every day like a new day, and what you had done yesterday is only still valid if you hold yourself and others to the same today.
You are constantly communicating through what you say and what you don't say. By what you do and what you say, by what you don't say and what you don't do communicates a message and lets people know how to treat you.

You may feel you are going to hurt someone's feelings if you tell them NO, or you don't want to 'kill the vibe', or you are not confrontational, or you'd genuinely like to please everyone. Whatever is your reasoning for not communicating how you really feel is a detriment to the situation. You are setting false expectations for people, you aren't being truthful to yourself, and you've given up the power over your life and leaving it to fate. Remember, your basic rights, they become critical in establishing the boundaries you want in your life.

When you don't communicate what you want, when you are not direct, then you are leaving the response up to fate. You are sitting at a craps table and you are rolling the dice hoping you win. The feeling of those winning chips in your hand can be so sweet and rewarding. Walking away from a losing table, however, knowing you've just spent your hard-earned money, can feel like your heart sinking into your chest. Fate is not a game you want to play with your life and your happiness.

Communication is key and it will allow you to walk away from the table winning. It doesn't always mean you may get the outcome you desired, but you will have been true and authentic to yourself, and that alone will keep your self-esteem high.

Think back to a time when you were a child and you were upset. You were flailing around on the floor sobbing uncontrollably. You were so worked up that the only sound you could come up with was the quivering noise that came as you tried to catch your breath. Your parents came running and desperately tried to figure out what was the matter.

They looked for signs of blood, signs of pain, signs of hurt, but all they found were tears. They kept asking, 'what's wrong- what's wrong?', but you couldn't stop crying. They were distraught, they didn't know how to help their precious little one, and they so desperately wanted to. They coddled you in their arms and they let you know how much they loved you. They told you it was going to be ok, even though they didn't know what was wrong, but they knew you were going to get through whatever it was. You were the only one that knew what happened, you were the only one that had the answer to their question.

'Tell us, what's wrong? Use your words.'

It's not always intuitive what is wrong or what is going on inside of you. You may have been crying in pain, you may have just swallowed your goldfish, you may have been crying because you missed your cousin. In order to get your message across you need to learn to communicate, it's not just understood.

When people know precisely what is happening then they know what to say or to do next. If you say nothing, then it's left guessing and intuition. The only person in the end who gets hurt is you.

People are not mind readers- use your words

I often hear how friends or clients get disappointed when they don't get what they want for their birthday or an anniversary. My first question is always 'did you say what you wanted?'

More often than not, the answer is 'well, not exactly, but I alluded to it'.

Seriously?! Since when did we start telepathically speaking with one another and it was actually effective communication? Even when you see relationships of people that have been together for decades that can finish each other's sentences, even they need to communicate to let the each other know what they want or don't want! In fact, the reason they've survived being in a relationship for so long is probably because they have had to learn to effectively communicate.

Let's look at why some relationships end or struggle.

- Needs weren't being bet
- Compatibility
- Different views on finances
- Lost the spark
- Too busy

Imagine if you started communicating your position and your boundary in all of those.

- Needs weren't being bet
  o What are your needs and how can they be fulfilled?
- Compatibility
  o Though you may not be into all the same hobbies and activities, where do you need or want support? Cherish the other person for what they have to offer, not what you have in common. Ask your partner what is important to him/her and be that support system
- Different views on finances

- Talk about your views on finances and come to a middle ground. You both may need to give up something (control, being a little flexible)
- Lost the spark
  - Talk about it. Sit down and see what you can do to rekindle the flame
- Too busy
  - If you think your partner is too busy, or you, for that matter, sit down and communicate what you need so you can adjust your boundaries. Maybe there are activities you can do together, or maybe you need to remove some or reprioritize for now

There are obviously many other causes of struggles, but you get the idea. Each causes a problem and each can have a solution or middle ground if you communicate. Communicating your boundaries let's people know where you stand on something, what your position is.

Don't just think something and hope the other person *knows* what to do. You open yourself up for disappointment and frustration, and your self-esteem can be compromised if your needs aren't getting fulfilled.

It's real simple, use your words.

Actions sometimes speak louder than words

There is an old adage that 'actions speak louder than words'. Yes, there are times when you need to communicate verbally, but sometimes the most effective form of communication is through your actions.

Ever heard anyone say they're going to stop smoking and it always seems to be next week or after the next holiday. At first, you get excited. You know smoking isn't good for their health and you know this would be a good step for your friend.

Next week comes and goes, and so does the next holiday- still smoking. The next time you see your friend the topic of quitting smoking comes up again. Same thing. Next week or after the next holiday.

Five years later you're still in the same loop of hearing your friend committing to quitting (and for the record, you never asked, or elicited promises from your friend). You've heard the promises and have become desensitized to them, so maybe it's time to see some action.

You'll believe it when you see it.

Sometimes you need to prove yourself through your actions, it may not come just by your words alone. You may be making a change in your life that no one is going to believe until it happens. Maybe you have led a life full of lies and deceit and you've committed to truth and honesty. Don't be surprised that some folks may be a bit skeptical, especially if you've said you were going to change in the past and you didn't. Holding true to your standards and having the right boundaries in place and showing commitment through your actions may be the exact thing to change people's perception.

It might sound different in your head than how it comes out

'That wasn't what I meant.'

'Yea, but that's how it came out.'

What you actually say and what you meant to say sometimes don't always align, and when that happens it might not be the message you wanted to communicate.

'If you think you're wearing all that makeup out of this house you have another thing coming!'

'But, Dad! All the girls wear makeup!'

'You look like a clown, go wash your face!'

Poor girl makes her way upstairs and her mom finds

her crying in the bathroom.

'Why does Dad think I'm ugly? I just want to be pretty like the rest of the girls.'

Dad never said anything about being ugly but telling his daughter she looks like a clown is subject to interpretation. Dad was merely referencing that clowns wear makeup, but that's entirely different than what his daughter heard.

What you say and what is heard may be two totally different messages, so choose your words wisely.

Be specific

When I arrived in Dallas I reacquainted with some of my mother's family that resided locally. My mom's cousin lived alone and I loved going and visiting with her. She was in her late 80's and it felt special to spend time with her because I didn't have very many people in my life that were in their 80's. Her son and his family also lived in Dallas and we decided to meet up one day for dinner at Spring Creek BBQ. I had seen it on the map and it appeared to be half way between our locations.

I remember standing outside for an hour while I waited for their arrival. Summers in Dallas are undeniably hot, and my face was melting, but for whatever reason I kept standing outside. I didn't have a cell phone number where I could reach them, and she didn't appear to be home since she wasn't answering her home phone.

I proceeded home finally and was concerned something might have happened, but I had no way to know. About 30 minutes after I got home I received a call from my lovely 'Aunt'. She told me she and her son had been waiting, so they ate and then came home.

Confused, I confirmed the location. "Spring Creek BBQ on Preston Road, right?"

"No dear, we were at "Spring Creek BBQ off 75."

I failed to know this was a chain restaurant and we both had the idea of where we were meeting, I should have been more specific. Conveying the address would have clarified the location, but I didn't know it was a chain restaurant. She went to the Spring Creek BBQ near her house that she frequents often so it's only natural that would be the location she went to.

Being specific clears up ambiguity or misinterpretation. Small details can be the game changer in a situation. Focus on being specific so you don't end up standing in the heat waiting for your dinner plans to come to fruition, only to go home hungry.

Overcommunicating is better than under communicating

It's not often that marriage counselors hear that a couple is running into problems because of overcommunicating, usually it's the opposite. We've addressed how under communication can be detrimental to relationships, but what about overcommunicating?

Think about the first time you drove some place and had to use your Global Positioning System (GPS) to navigate there. You'd sit in your driveway, load the address and start your route. You knew some of the way (how to get out of your neighborhood, which major highway to get on), but you were not 100% on how to get to the final destination. After four or five times of using the GPS you felt comfortable enough to navigate there on your own. You realized, however, there were a couple of points along the way that you needed to turn it on because you were uncertain. Finally, after 10 times of driving the same route you were able to get to your end destination without the GPS telling you where to turn left or right.

Even though you knew part of your route the first time, you programmed the address in before you even left. Eventually, you didn't need that level of communication and you could navigate on your own.

You weren't bothered by the GPS telling you turns you already knew, because there were turns you didn't know. But, eventually you knew the path and it wasn't necessary to keep getting directions.

Overcommunicating can be effective in getting your message across, and if you're consistent with your messaging then it's good reinforcement. You need to assess your situation to determine when someone doesn't need that level of communication (because it can become overbearing if it is used when it doesn't need to be), but as a general rule of thumb it's better to overcommunicate than under.

Repetition creates a pattern

As we discussed before, being consistent with your messaging will help to create a pattern. If you communicate one message one day and a different message to the same situation the next, then you've muddied the waters and created confusion on what your boundaries truly are.

Imagine your kids asked you if it was ok to have a cookie for breakfast (let's assume this was a Tuesday). You are thinking to yourself that you probably shouldn't give your kids sugar as their first meal of the day so you tell them no. The next day, same question, same answer. On Thursday, they ask again and you allow them. Friday, the kids go get a cookie without asking. To them, it was fine yesterday, it must be fine every day. It was the answer they were waiting for, they got it, and now to them it's the rule. You see them with the cookies and you are beside yourself.

What ownership do you take in the situation?

If you communicate different boundaries then they become confusing or subjective to whomever is interpreting them. Can you fault the kids for thinking it was ok to eat cookies before they went to school since they did it the day before? Now, maybe you just needed to put a stipulation in there stating that this was a 'special treat' for something they did, and not to expect it every day. This would level-set that it was not the new norm but in fact a reward they got for a special event or good behavior. Now, that might communicate that good behavior equals cookies, which may or may not be the message you want to communicate, but you can work through that if it comes up again.

Repetition creates a pattern, so make sure you are not only creating the pattern of behavior that you want but that you hold true to it. Otherwise, you can't fault others for misinterpreting you if you are in fact loosey-goosey with it yourself.

Be prepared for the response

Communication can be vulnerable, it opens you up to criticism. You are communicating a message and whatever you put out there, you have to be prepared for any response. Whether verbally or through your actions, you are constantly communicating a message even when you might not be aware of it. You need to become aware of the message you are sending, and don't be afraid to put it out there. It's communicating how you feel, it's communicating what you want, it's communicating what you need, it's communicating what you are striving for, it's communicating what you want to achieve, it's communicating your emotions, and it's communicating your desires.

Your message might not always be well received, so be prepared for the response- armor yourself with boundaries to protect yourself from any rejection.

Rejection can hurt. I get it. So arm yourself appropriately.

Don't let fear stop you

What if you never acted on that 'million-dollar idea' because you didn't want to fail?

What if you were too afraid to speak up about your life story but you knew it could help someone?

What if you wanted to go skydiving but you let fear get in the way of one of the most exhilarating life experiences?

Imagine if you never proposed because you were afraid

of the response. What if you ended up losing the love of your life and the possibility of a life and family together because of that fear?

What if at 80-years old you looked back and wondered about every area you didn't act on because of fear? What if you wished you had done everything because you realize now that there is no reward without risk. Your wisdom now also tells you that there is no failure, life offers course corrections and lessons.

If you don't communicate because you are fearful of the response or rejection, then we will never be able to experience some of the true joys in life: love, deep friendship, winning, having a solid set of values, self-love and respect, respect from others and happiness. We cannot let fear dictate our decisions or if we choose to communicate.

I think back to the time several jobs ago when I communicated to my boss that I was not interested in the job he had slotted me for. I was bold in making a statement that went against his thoughts and opinions, but I remained true to me. Had I shifted into that role, I would have most likely spent years doing something I was not passionate about doing and I would have done nothing to advance my career, which was my ultimate goal. The response was that I ultimately got laid-off, and I was prepared for that response. I felt better about myself because I stood up for myself, and I believe that my higher power had a different idea of what I should be doing. I walked out of the office that day with my head held high and I was not afraid to be truthful and honest not only to myself, but also to my boss.

Communicate what you believe to be true and honest. Don't let fear get in your way or you will be inhibiting your own progress.

Don't give up

Ever seen a kid ride a bike and just crash to the ground with a disastrous spill? What do you tell the poor thing as you go over and wipe the tears away? Do you say 'give up, you'll never be any good'?

No, you don't.

You tell this kid to get up and try again. You let him know that everything will be ok, and he'll get it, but he'll never get it if he gives up.

Don't give up on yourself when you fall. Don't get discouraged and retreat back into your safe little hole. No one ever made forward momentum by stopping.

Shift gears

"I have told you 10 times not to slam the door!"

Sound familiar? I see myself running out of the house

of our cabin in Vermont and my Dad telling me not to slam the door.

Just because you communicate doesn't always mean you are going to get your way, but that doesn't mean you are out of options. The threat of not getting Ben & Jerry's ice cream could certainly correct my behavior if I didn't listen! That's one way!

I think back to the time I told my boss I didn't want the position he had in mind for me. I even told him what areas I was interested in. Sure, my intent was that he would take those suggestions and find me a role that I could have slid into, but instead my position got cut and so did I. No big deal, I shifted and moved on.

I think back to when I had a friend that wasn't respecting people's money or time. Considering I was one of those people I said something because I was directly impacted. I was not going to be taken advantage of, disrespected, or be emotionally exhausted because of her actions so I said something on more than one occasion.   In the end, I walked away from the friendship because she was not someone I aligned with or wanted to have in my life. I said my piece and all she did was get nasty with me, it was her way or the highway. That was perfectly fine with me, I took the highway and I was true and authentic to myself. My mental boundaries kicked in, there are 7+ billion people in this world and if she and I can't get along, then it's zero loss to me. I lost 1/7,000,000,000 of a person's possible friendships in this world- that's so negligible on the scale that it's about a zero in the grand scheme. No loss there, and my self-esteem remained intact because I stayed true to myself and didn't allow a bully to knock me over.

You can shift gears in life. If that means finding a different way of communicating, moving on from a situation, or even walking away from a friendship, you have that choice to shift gears.

Communicating does not mean you will get the desired outcome, but you *will* remain true and authentic to yourself if you do. Know that you may need to pull on one of your other boundaries to help you get through the situation, maybe emotional, spiritual or mental. In the end, it's a fundamental right (as long as you are not harming anyone), so do not shy away because you are fearful of what others may say or think. Knowing that communication is paramount it needs to be part of your journey as you delve into establishing your life as you want it to be directed.

We've learned a lot up to this point about setting standards, why we need boundaries and what boundaries look like, now let's pull it all together.

Chapter 16: Pulling it together

We've covered lots of information, and I hope as you've gone through the chapters that you've started to generate some true and honest thoughts about where you are, opinions and have some semblance of where you are at or want to be. Now, let's start to pull all these ideas and topics we've discussed together.

First, remember how you want your life to look is a choice and it's entirely up to you to not only decide, but to execute. Life is a series of choices to make and paths to take. Those paths may lead to positive outcomes and some may lead you right down the path to a place you might feel you are at now (mentally or physically), but it's entirely up to you to decide where you want to end up.

Unanticipated and unplanned events are going to happen. Even then, you choose which mental path you take to deal with the situation. Really grasping the principle of choice is foundational. If you think you *have to* panic, that's false. Again I'll say, panic, fear, and anxiety do not produce results. Results produce results. How you choose to feel is up to you. If you are anything but happy and content then you are not where you could be and you should choose a different mental path (mindset).

Second, use what you can and cannot control to be your guide to narrow down where you focus your energy. If you are focused on what you cannot control then you are not setting yourself up for success. I don't mean neutral situations (you think some puppy is cute but you don't control the animal), I'm talking about a situation where it impacts you in some capacity or you've emotionally attached yourself to it (such as a pandemic, a politician, a coworker, a driver, someone who did you wrong, a comment, an action, a disagreement, your future).

If you are focused on things that are outside of your control then you are wasting energy. If you can't control it, then it's useless to exert energy. I found that not only was I wasting energy by focusing on things outside of my control, but I also found myself usually angry, anxious, fearful, or upset when I was focused on these things.

Next, think about someone in your life you admire. Maybe it's a mentor or someone close to you, or maybe it's someone you admire from a distance. This should be someone you respect and look up to. What are the traits about this person that makes them attractive or likable? How do they act with others? How's their family life? Are they spiritual? What's their work ethic? Do they give back to the community? How do you resonate with their message?

Conversely, think of someone you have little to no respect for. What are those characteristics you don't want to carry over into your own life? Do they talk down to others? Are they unreliable? Do they always put a negative spin on a situation and try to get others to agree with them? Do they gossip and spread rumors? Do they have attributes you don't want in your own life?

To be clear, there may be someone in your life that you respect in some areas and not in others, people don't have to fit in one category or another. If you want to be that respectable leader, then having consistency across your life will garner deeper respect from people, and I'd encourage you to have values and traits that align across all areas of your life.

When you see positive aspects in others that you admire and want to emulate, GO FOR IT! But you may also see other aspects in those same people that you don't want in your life, so stay away from those parts. Pick and choose the best of what you want your life to look like and what you want to be known for.

Sometimes when we see the behaviors in others that we like or dislike then we have a better idea of how we want to set up our own lives. That may even include those little things that sometimes go unnoticed. I always appreciated when I was a guest at someone's house, and they put out a towel and bar of soap for me. It communicated to me that they put some thought into my stay and wanted to make me feel comfortable. Now, I try to do the same with my guests because of the way it made me feel. Observe and replicate, take on those traits that make you feel good. If someone has characteristics you'd like to emulate, there's no sense in reinventing the wheel, might as well learn from their life. It's also highly complementary. Imagine if someone came to you and told you that by watching you and following in your steps they were also able to find happiness. Imitation is one of the highest forms of flattery.

Now, write a generalized list of standards (set of behaviors/values) of what you think your life should look like (even if they're areas you need to work on). Maybe that looks like:

- Honest
- Dependable
- Loyal
- Positive
- Opportunistic
- Happy
- Respectable
- Financially independent
- Financially responsible
- Thoughtful

Lay out a list of characteristics of how you would want someone to characterize you, put your ideal down on paper. Think of those people you admire, what traits about them do you want people to characterize you as?

Go back to that smiley-face poster of 200 feelings. Go through each one of those and think about what comes to mind. You are sitting on an arsenal of relevant examples in your life of situations that you can draw from. Yes, it's OK to look at others and see what you like or dislike about their lives, but no one has gone through what you have.

Using your generalized list above, along with your basic rights and feelings, list out specific standards and goals you want in your life. Think back to the chapters of emotional, physical, sexual, spiritual, mental, intellectual and time boundaries and what came to mind as you read through them. It might look like:

- You are a priority
- You can put yourself first
- Work will not consume all your time
- A healthy work/life balance is a requirement
- Your emotional needs matter
- You are not willing to be an afterthought in a relationship
- Your higher power is a priority
- Remaining faithful to your partner is paramount
- Arriving on time is not always necessary
- Sleep is a priority
- You want to target eating healthy 85% of the time

- You don't mind if people touch you when they talk, if they are the type to talk with their hands
- Making deliverables at work accurately and on time is important
- Remain carefree
- Quality over quantity for friendships
- Paying bills on-time
- Having an income is a priority
- Live a purpose driven life
- Exercise is a priority

When I went through this exercise I wrote down areas in my life where I did not feel fulfilled or areas that gave me anxiety. These were the easy situations to go after. If I could identify dysfunction, then it needed to be addressed.

These areas included:

- Work
- Sleep
- Dating
- Friendships
- Money
- Self-Image

Think through what areas of dissatisfaction you have and assess why you aren't satisfied. What boundaries do you need to establish in your life to get you to your standards?

Then think through real situations and began

identifying and applying the standards and setting boundaries.

My work/life balance went entirely off kilter

I'm not sure when it happened, but I found myself thrown into my job and it consuming my life. When I decided I was a priority, sleep mattered, happiness mattered, I found that my time in the office did not align with the desires for my life!

I would look around the office and see people leaving at a structured time and yet I was staying until I felt like it was time to wrap up. It didn't matter to me if I had to go in on the weekend, I would do whatever it took. All this did was keep me bound to an office and keep me from things that made me truly happy (friends, hobbies, etc.).

I decided I was going to start working a standard 40-hour work week and boy did I start to feel better immediately! I had so much more time in my week to do things for me!

Sleep needed to get prioritized!
The older I get the harder it is to do well on a few hours of sleep a night. For years, I went with having 4-5 hours of sleep a night and I was fine the next day. I

would catch up on sleep on the weekend and I would coast with minimal sleep during the week.

Having studied health for so many years, I know the benefits of getting sleep, yet I never adhered to it. It was time to make it a priority.

I gave myself a bedtime.

There I was in my 30's and what I fought as a kid I desired as an adult; bedtime and sleep! In order to achieve this, I had to hold myself to that bedtime so that meant making changes or concessions in my life. Well worth it, I cannot imagine going backwards and getting that little sleep ever again.

I had some friendships that I was more into than they were

I have been blessed with a lot of really great people in my life, I have never struggled to meet people. What I realized, however, was that I valued many of them as friends when really they were acquaintances.

Looking at my standards I realized I was not putting myself first or finding enjoyment when it was constantly me initiating the conversations. I didn't drop these people from my life, but I did decide to not invest my time into always seeing how they were doing. It had to be a 2-way street of interest in each other's life for me to want to invest my time. Otherwise, it was me throwing my energy into a wishing well and hoping something would come from it. I was fine with shifting these people to acquaintances and focusing my attention on the people that were interested in maintaining a deeper level of friendship.

I was disrespectful to myself

I most certainly needed a boundary with myself. I was so mean to myself all the time! I cannot believe I would entertain some of the self-deprecation when I would never imagine saying any of those things to anyone else.

It didn't make me happy to call myself fat, to tell myself I wasn't worth it, to not support myself. I needed to change my self-talk to align with the standard I wanted in my life. I began immediately flipping the script and telling myself that I was worth it and I was enough- no more disrespecting.

Once I started to be mindful of areas where I was unhappy and the standards I wanted to center my life around, I became more aware of what was happening in my life. I started to pay attention to cause and effect and the role I played in my situation. I found myself to be much happier just by setting standards in my life and making myself a priority. Self-hate, negativity, anxiety, panic, fear and pessimism were no longer going to be acceptable.

Sometimes, we don't know what boundaries we need to set until we have actually gone through the situation, at which point we then need to step back and assess where boundaries need to be established. Your standards will be your guide (along with focusing on what you can and cannot control) and help to define those boundaries when the situation arises.

This exercise is not a one-and-done. Make self-reflecting a priority and continuously assess what is working and not working. Life happens, things change, priorities change, we get older, people come in and out of our lives. We need to constantly be assessing what is working and what is not working and what needs to be tweaked. You're an adult, so make the adult assessment over the course of your life and get real with yourself. If you are not in tune with yourself at this level, then you are at risk for new situations overrunning your life.

Standards will be the guidelines for your boundaries, and the boundaries end up being your playbook for your life. First assess how you want to be treated and what you truly value, and then create those bumpers on your bowling lane of life to ensure you stay within your lane. You keep out what doesn't belong and you keep in what serves you.

I cannot emphasize enough how critical it is to learn to

self-reflect. You need to get into your own head and see what is going on. If you leave it up to chance then you have no power over your life. Think about it, you are literally that Venom F5, but if you don't self-reflect and tap into your power then you are driving around in a $2M vehicle like it's a Nissan Maxima.
Write things down so you can visualize what your life might look like on paper. You don't have to define all of the paths you will take or the decisions you will make, these are the aims, the goals. The specifics come when you start to maneuver through life getting to your goals- those are the boundaries.

Let's look at what some situations look like where we apply a standard and boundary.

- **Situation**: You're asked to take a lateral move at work that does not interest you
  - **Standard**: Live a purpose driven life
  - **Boundary**: Say no because the work does not fulfill your purpose
- **Situation**: You're asked to take a lateral move at work that does not interest you
  - **Standard**: Happiness is a priority
  - **Boundary**: Say no because this job is not one that you have any desire to put your energy in to or a team you want to work with. You foresee yourself not being happy
- **Situation**: You're asked to take a lateral move at work that does not interest you

- o **Standard**: Retire at 60
- o **Boundary**: Say no because this job will not move you toward your financial goals to retire at 60
- **Situation**: You're asked to take a lateral move at work that does not interest you
  - o **Standard**: Pay bills on-time
  - o **Boundary**: You weigh the options of taking this job because it would allow you to continue to pay your bills on time if your current role gets eliminated

All are the same situation and depending on which standard you apply could change the boundary you establish for the situation.

Establishing these standards will help you to grow and develop. It's like planting the seed in the ground and then letting it grow. If you never plant the seed, you will never grow anything. Once you plant a seed, you then need to make sure it has water to make it grow or it will remain a seed. Sometimes you'll need to adjust the soil, pull weeds, water extra, or maybe even replant the plant, but as long as you are tending to it consistently then there is a higher chance the plant is going to flourish. You'll figure out the right mix when you self-reflect.

You already have a lot to pull from in your life, so start with those areas where you feel discontent and think about why. What could have been done differently, and what standards did that go against? You might not have ever thought about it before as being a standard in your life but write it down now.

There are a lot of decision paths and influences that impact decisions. Staying true to your core standards is where you'll find yourself with higher self-esteem, greater respect from others, and satisfaction in life. Don't beat yourself up if you make the wrong decision, just self-reflect, learn and move on. Don't try to map out your every move, that's not only impossible but that's entirely too rigid. In the example above I had four of the same situations where I pulled on different standards to make my decision tree. Don't overthink life and remember that going with your gut is a really powerful tool. Since we've established you cannot fail then the worst that can happen is you learn a valuable life lesson. When you sit down and do this exercise it starts to raise the level of awareness and accountability you have with your life. Leaving it to chance is like planting that seed and hoping it grows, it takes lots of work along the way.

Doing a daily personal inventory is a good practice to get into, where you are constantly assessing what you could have done better and aim to improve the next time. When you lose that connection with yourself then that negativity can start to creep in and take over before you even know it.

You have to start somewhere, so just start growing and then build on your list. You have a choice, let go of what you can't control, determine your standards, and start to place boundaries in your life. Use people you admire (or don't admire) as a place to start. Determine what you want to emulate in your life and build out from there.

Chapter 17: How do you enforce boundaries?

You've gone years without enforcing your boundaries, so where you do start? Let's look at an example of a company in disarray and how boundaries can help bring order out of chaos. It may sound a bit like a case study from some MBA program, but trust me, it happened.

Imagine you get hired as a CEO for a struggling company. The stocks were dropping, morale was low, attrition was high, and the overall vision wasn't clear to you or much of the current leadership. You interviewed each one of your direct reports and there was a semblance of a story that painted the picture of how the company hit a slump, but no one had a definitive answer. The other observation you made was that synergy across the departments didn't exist. It was as if they were independent departments that did not operate cross-functionally.

The Information Technology Department (IT) didn't understand the business well enough to develop a software to support customer's needs, or at least that's what the Operations Department would say. IT had their own idea of what they should be developing, and even though it should be a decision driven by Operations or maybe even Business Development, IT would go buy whatever they wanted and spend their unlimited budget doing so. Since no one understood IT, they always seemed to come up with an astronomical budget, which no one contested. Even though the company hadn't sold a software product in years, they managed to keep 150 developers on staff, although no one was quite sure what they were doing or how their jobs were justified.

The Finance Department operated like they were in the 1970's. They were the biggest bubble of the entire company. Paper invoices would be received and get paid on the spot without proper validation from the business. No one appeared to understand budgeting, or at least come forward with a feasible and reasonable plan. The company missed its financial targets every year because they didn't forecast all variables that go into budgeting (capital investments, new business, growth, automation/innovation to name a few). No one seemed to track or care when sites closed down-Finance would continue to pay the bills. Though minimal processes were in place, undoubtedly they would fail an audit because of the lack of structure and adherence to any level of repetition within their organization. It was no surprise the company was in financial trouble.

The Business Development team was entirely disconnected with the business, especially Operations and IT (the most critical departments to understand). IT was building software solutions to meet business needs, but no one took the time to understand the vision to sell it forward. They were out there selling the products they thought the company offered, without having a grounded knowledge of what the business was truly offering. They were selling anything they could, and usually it ended up being marginal deals versus landing the big wins. The previous CEO would consistently set unrealistic sales targets, so the entire company would miss their bonuses year-after-year. The sales team seemed to spend more than they would make back, must be nice to expense all travel, meals and entertainment and not be held accountable for actually selling anything.

Operations was doing the best they could to support the customer. The problem was they were off doing their own thing and not collaborating with the headquarters when making decisions. They signed their own contracts, they bought their own equipment, and grossly wasted money at every turn. Based off consumption, it appeared many of the locations must have been buying supplies for their employees to take home for their kids, the spending on supplies was astronomical. Although typically IT supported, Operations kept independently trying different innovative solutions to improve the business. Nothing proved successful and money kept getting wasted on all these menial attempts to achieve process improvements or financial gains.

The Human Resources Department (HR) was centrally located and never got out to have face time with any of the departments. Every complaint the employees had seemed to fall on deaf ears, HR was a black hole. HR seemed to be the team that laid off employees, that was the only time they ever became visible.

The legal team was another black hole full of expensive lawyers that sat up next to the executives. No one knew what they did, but they certainly weren't involved in the contract process. Like HR, they would choose to show their face when something juicy came up (or when more employees needed to be laid off).

Imagine you walk into this and you are told you need to turn the ship around. Overwhelming, there is so much to be done, but you're up for the challenge. In fact, you love challenges. You'd rather go into something that presents an opportunity for improvement instead of a well-oiled machine because you find it more stimulating and rewarding. That's why they are paying you the big bucks.

Where do you start? First, you need buy-in from your direct reports, the leaders of the company. No more segregated departments, there will be just one cohesive company. You have an offsite meeting after you've spent a month talking to the investors, listening and observing the company's antics.

You've determined there are some clear gaps. No one takes ownership, everyone points fingers, no one has a clear vision of the company's direction and each department seems to have their own rules and way of operating. Today that stops. You let your team know that they will all become a cohesive unit and that starts with enhancing the collaboration.

There is also structure and processes that need to be developed. The company is no longer going to operate as independent fiefdoms. Processes will be standardized across the company and enforced. If anyone goes outside of these processes, if people start signing their own contracts, then there will be serious penalties.

Lastly, company culture needs to be addressed. There needs to be a reward system for the high performers, there needs to be local events to celebrate the employees, and there needs to be catered lunches from time to time.

You know you have a thousand more things you want to address, but you start there and you'll bring the leadership back in 6 months to address progress to date and the next round of changes. It's an uphill climb, but you know you can do it. It may take eliminating some folks that don't align with the vision or are not in support, but those are the hard decisions you're paid to make.

In your world you are your own CEO, and it's time to address your life. It's time to make it a rock-solid company that people respect, including yourself, and you need to establish boundaries to get there. Just like the CEO in this company, you don't have to tackle it all at once, but you need to get started.

Assessing your situation

Baselining your life is first. Focus on areas with negativity or angst. These are the easy areas you will first want to work on to improve.

You are reconnecting with yourself, so it might take some soul-searching to get here. They say, 'Rome wasn't built in a day' and neither will you. This is going to take time to really dig in and fix the gaps and make you solid, but you will get there if you keep at it.

Get into your quiet space, grab a note pad and think about how you want your company to look (your life). What does your empire look like? What values do you hold? What's your objective? How do you want to be remembered? Think about that person you admire. What are the traits and values that person holds that you want to have people look at you and see?

Consistency

Consistency helps create clarity and predictablity. It's confusing to others when you are uber liberal in some areas and uber conservative in others. It's probably equally confusing for yourself if you are all over the map. Me personally, yes, I do have some political thoughts and ideas that are a bit more liberal and a bit more conservative, but in general I'm about the middle of the road on most things.

People know me as someone who isn't afraid to speak her mind, to stand up for myself, to be trustworthy, to be tenacious, to be all in or not in at all. If I was trustworthy about some things but not for others, then this would create doubt in the circle around me and it would tarnish my credibility. If I was sometimes afraid to speak my mind, then certain leadership opportunities may not have presented themselves to me.

Having consistency, having a common thread across your attributes and values, will help minimize the confusion and make it more predictable when people are interacting with you. You don't want to cause confusion, it should be easy for them.

This is your branding

Think of this entire book as your branding. You are creating the image you want to leave with everyone. For any business, branding is key, and that is no different than how you need to look at how you are viewed. Branding is what makes a memorable impression and sets the expectation with your 'customers' or 'clients' on what they can expect.

This again reinforces why you do not want a confusing brand. Like the company in disarray at the beginning of this chapter, Business Development said yes to anything. They also weren't meeting their sales. Why? They didn't have brand recognition, they didn't have a niche they went after, they just said yes to everything.

Branding is key, so uphold it as it is worth its weight in gold.

Clarification with people in your life

Especially for the people in your close circle, I'd suggest having a clear discussion with them if things are going to change. It's a sign of strength to admit when you are wrong or when you need to make improvements in your life. If you sat your family down and said 'I want to be a better person, and I know I need to work on some areas in my life to get there. There are going to be some changes that are going to happen, and I want to show you through my actions that I can in fact be that person I know I'm destined to be.' They may not fully understand or be at that same level of self-awareness, but at least they will know that things are going to change. It shows courage and strength. Remember those emotional and mental boundaries. Be prepared for people not to understand, be prepared for some backlash. If that happens, then you'll have prepped your brain to block the negativity.

I remember when my parents made me buy my first car instead of giving me one. Let's say I fought back, stomped my feet and said it was unfair? As the parents, they knew that having a car payment would teach me financial responsibility, it would teach me about paying bills, might reduce my chance of driving recklessly, and I would be better prepared for the future when I was out of their house and on my own. As a teenager, this is probably not where my head went to as I was justifying it, but I realized as an adult that I was taught these skills because of the wise decisions my parents made.

Not everyone will have the vision you have for your boundaries, but if you set them up with honesty and integrity, if you truly believe in what you are doing, then arm your mental boundaries to protect you for from people who don't see your vision. The key is to not let your boundaries slip just because someone does not see them your way (in cases where you are upholding your integrity and acting with honesty). It may take some clarification, but just keep at it.

Show through example

As we discussed, some traits are shown through example, like trust. You certainly could sit your family down and tell them you want to be more trustworthy, but until you prove it, it's just something you want to do. If there is a broken relationship due to distrust, then it could take some time to mend and repair. After some time, they will understand that you are no longer cutting corners, cheating people, lying, but in fact leading a life that is full of trust and honesty.

This isn't going to happen overnight, it's going to take time. There could be healing that people need to go through because of your actions. If they have been burned over and over then it is going to take time for them to gain that level of trust in you, and it might take time for them to even like to respect you again. The damage can be repaired, but it will take consistent examples to turn the ship around, and don't expect that it is going to happen overnight.

Even without having any bad habits or past to overcome, actions are more powerful than words. It's how you show the world you mean business.

No pointing fingers, take ownership

Remember, you take ownership of your life. You are your own CEO and what happens is your responsibility. But again, if you arm your mind with the right mental boundaries then you are in a position to have everything be a positive, because you have chosen to take the optimistic vantage point. You will look for the lessons in the challenges. You choose to grow rather than to wither.

You are not here to place blame on anyone or anything, you take accountability for your life. You've placed strong emotional boundaries in place to keep yourself calm so you are well positioned for anything that comes your way. You react maturely, and if you are knee-jerking to a situation and overreacting then you need to enhance your emotional boundaries.

There is no more:

- I can't do this
- It was because of my upbringing
- He/She did it to me
- I give up
- I'll never get there
- It's his/her fault
- I don't have enough money
- I don't have enough experience
- I don't know where to begin
- It's just too hard
- I was never taught how to

No more victim, you're the boss, you lead the charge.

"Victims make excuses. Leaders deliver results." – Robin Sharma

Penalties might need to be enforced

There are times where penalties are needed to enforce boundaries. Life might seem easier if there were no consequences enforced, but there are times and places where they reinforce positive behaviors and are necessary.

Let's say your child keeps coming in at 12am when the curfew is 11pm. You have the conversation a couple of time but no behavior changes. If this continues to happen, then maybe it's time to take away driving privileges or phone rights. Taking something away helps to reinforce the importance of the behavior you are putting boundaries around. This may not be the route to take in all cases, but where appropriate penalties may help get your point across.

We all know that murder is not acceptable in any state. Not only will you go to prison, but there is a chance to have the death penalty enforced due to your actions. This level of penalty exists to deter people from the egregious act of murder.

It's not always a penalty that needs to be enforced, it could be your response to the situation that gets the point across. Go back to your basic rights. You have the right to say no. You have the right to walk away.

I recently started talking to someone I had met on a dating app and we had some good conversations, at least for the first week. After getting to know each other a bit he let me know that he had a busy few months ahead of him. We continued to talk and I believe we both enjoyed each other's conversations, we connected well. But, he was so busy that we didn't get much deeper in our conversations after that first week, and there were times he said he would make time to talk and he would consistently have to cancel or he fell asleep.

Now, let's assume all of this was true, which I believe it was. He was upfront with me that he was going to be busy in the upcoming months and knowing his industry and what was happening in the world, I understood the demand.

By the same token, I also didn't like the fact that I kept getting canceled on (or that he'd fall asleep and I'd be hopeful we would talk). I am fine with supporting someone's dream, and trust me, I'm so busy myself that I don't want someone zapping all my time. But, I have a boundary in place that I didn't feel good about and I told him to call me when he had more time in his schedule to make for me, and I moved on.

We both communicated where we were at, and he told me he respected that position and he agreed that he wasn't making the proper time, because he didn't have the time to give. We talked through it like adults and that was that.

I had to be comfortable with enforcing my own boundary. Even though I enjoyed chatting, I felt like he was far too busy to put time in to get to know each other and I didn't just want to be a pen-pal. I knew going in that he was busy, I gave it a try, and I backed out when it started to cross my boundary where I didn't feel important.

You have to enforce boundaries, otherwise boundaries do not exist. Enforcing is not always a direct penalty, it can be that walking away, or you may have to tell someone no. Remember, people are not mind readers, they are not going to know what is going on with you unless you tell them. Don't let things fester and boil and then explode on them, that won't be good for anyone. Be an adult, use your words, and talk through what you are feeling and experiencing. They will respect your communication much more than they will respect you blowing up because you harbored a bunch of feelings inside as your boundaries were breached.

You enforce boundaries by being clear, discussing with others, following through with your actions, taking responsibility for your life and your actions, and enforcing your basic rights and penalties. If boundaries are not enforced and you merely keep them in your head then you are destined for disappointment. This is where you'll see your self-esteem be compromised because your expectation and reality do not match.

Define your boundaries and put them into use. Everyone in your life, including you, will benefit when you do.

Chapter 18: Recognizing when boundaries are off kilter

Boundaries can be tricky. Sometimes we don't always know how to approach a situation until we've gone through it. Knowing what our standards are will help dictate what the boundaries look like, but even in an entirely new situation it may take a little more thought as you navigate through it to make sure you are staying true to your beliefs.

You may get through a situation and question some of your moves, or some of the behaviors that entered your space.

You have established happiness as a standard in your life. You know that when you get anxious, frustrated or negative that none of those purposes help you get to your end state goal. I know for many of us, having lived through the COVID-19 crisis, that many went into a state of panic and fear. We turned on the news and we saw the death toll rising and we got paralyzed by the unknown. Before we knew it, that standard of happiness wasn't being met because our boundaries were off kilter. We got sucked into the pandemonium and before we knew it we lost sight of where we were going.

So, how do you recognize when your boundaries are off-kilter and you're getting off track?

Follow your gut

Let that gut be your guide. Remember the power you hold in your gut. If it starts to feel off balance or out of whack, then you probably are.

I know that when I am bloated, this is a telltale sign that something in my diet isn't right or I'm dealing with some reaction. Maybe I ate too much fiber, maybe I'm constipated, and maybe I ate too much salt, or drank carbonated drinks that caused bubbles in my stomach. Whatever it may be, I know that if my gut doesn't feel good that I've done something wrong.

If you are in the middle of a situation and your gut alarm goes off, you probably need to assess why that is happening and what you need to do to remedy it. Your gut is powerful and will send you signals, so use it as your radar. If it doesn't feel right- investigate.

Self-reflect

Staying in tune with your thoughts and actions is a true sign of maturity. It means you have self-awareness and that what you do matters.

Most days, I try to think about what I did well that day and what I could have done better. I focus mostly on what I could have done better, and focus on improving in those areas.

I try to stay positive. I try to remain calm when situations happen. I try to focus on what I can control and let go of what I cannot control. I try to stay in tune with my higher power. I try to be a good sister. I try to be a good daughter. I try to....I try to....I try to. There are so many things to try to and to balance that if we are not reflecting and cognizant of our thoughts, actions and behaviors then we could easily get off track.

Have you ever gone grocery shopping for a specific list of items but you didn't write anything down? Let's say it was for a dinner party and you needed some specific ingredients to make the bread rise, the sauce thicken, and the dessert to set-up. You go down all of the aisles and you try so hard to remember what you needed. Your grocery cart is full and you get down to the checkout line and you go through the list in your mind one last time. Your total comes to $102.70. Surely you must have everything you needed at that price!

As you walk out the grocery store you get this feeling that you missed something, but you can't think of what it might be. Your entire ride home you have that same feeling, and it's not until you start preparing the meal that you realize that you missed two key ingredients.

It's easy to miss an ingredient if we aren't paying attention or if we're not reading from a list. Life isn't scripted, so we are doing the best we can as we go throughout the day. The way we will know if we missed an ingredient is if we stop and reflect. Where did your gut tell you it was off, or what in your heart did you know you could have done better.

I had a CEO ask me one time what was one of the best changes I made in my life and I said 'self-refection'. The act of doing this often gave me a better level of self-awareness and it helped me to make continuous improvements.

Are you focused on what you can control?

Remember, let what you can and cannot control be your guide. If you are self-reflecting or being cognizant in the moment and you find that you are focused on areas that you cannot control- then you need to adjust your boundaries. You need to focus only on those things you can control.

Looking at the pandemic of the COVID-19 crisis, there were so many things that we just simply could not control. The death rate, the cure, the layoffs, the shelter-in-place, the stock market, the missed vacations, the graduations- so many things that could not be controlled. Are you placing your time and attention into those kinds of areas? Or, are you focused on those things you can control: watching your budget, spending quality time with your family, picking up a hobby, self-improvement?

Focus on those items you do control versus what is entirely out of your control. Your boundaries should be around what you do control, so if you are outside of that then your boundaries are off-kilter.

Are you discontent?

Are you feeling disappointed at how things are going in your life? Is there a general sense that you are just not where you want to be?

Maybe you have started to notice that more people are taking advantage of you, maybe even your own family. It's frustrating you and you just aren't going to sleep with a good feeling. You feel discontent and you might not even know why.

This is where you need to take a step back and really assess the root cause and see if there are things that you could or should be doing in your life that will ultimately address those areas of discontent.

Teenage years are not always the easiest time of life. They're starting to experience their independence and they seem to have gone from these adorable children that would run up and hug you and now they barely want to be seen in public with you. How did this happen? Your 'little princess' turned into someone like a reality TV show personality from the Kardashian's, and you don't have anything in common! You miss your little girl, and it seems the only way you can connect is if you give in to whatever she asks. But, when you do, you don't always feel good about it. She's always asking for money, and she's barely getting the grades you'd expect.

Your boundaries are off kilter!

First, some of this is a stage, I went through it myself. It took me until I went to college for my perspective of my parents to change. They started to change in my mind from 'parents that kept a rule book' to being actual humans. It's just perspective, and teenagers are just trying to figure it out themselves, don't take it personally. See where you can connect on a different level, and hold true to your values that you believe in, even if they don't. Engage those mental boundaries to help weather the storm during these tumultuous years and stay true to you.

Enforcing what is right isn't always easy, but you need to stand behind your decisions. When you get push-back, self-reflect and make sure your standards and boundaries are proper, balanced and meaningful or if they need adjustment. In the long run, you will garner more respect, even if that's not acknowledged right away.

Let discontent and discomfort be your guide that you need to put boundaries in place or review them and strengthen your mind.

Do people keep crossing your boundaries?

Do you find that people continue to cross your boundaries? You've established an honest policy at work yet employees keep stealing or lying. You've talked to your spouse about wanting to spend time together but it never happens. You keep feeling disrespected in your own home.

If you feel your boundaries are being crossed, then guess what? Enforce them!

If you are feeling your boundaries are being crossed, then they are off kilter and you need to re-establish. If you've allowed boundaries to become 'loose' then you need to tighten them, or maybe even establish them for the first time.

As I said earlier, if you have reasonable boundaries and someone, even a loved one, refuses to honor them, then you know what you need to do to protect yourself.

Are you angry, paranoid, frustrated? Are you anything but happy?

If you are anything but happy, then this is a sign you need to dig into your brain and put up the boundaries. Go back to the chapter *Armed by Mental Boundaries* and really learn about putting up a shield when negativity starts to creep in. This doesn't mean that you cannot feel sad about a loss, or fear about a diagnosis, but it means you need to stay closely connected to your thoughts and make sure you are keeping them on track.

It's easy for boundaries to get off kilter, there are so many things happening in this world that we can easily lose sight of a goal, an objective, or let doubt and negativity creep in. Recognizing the warning signs will help you stay on track so you can have a more consistent state of happiness. Let your gut, let your feelings, let your emotions be your guide and evaluate your life when you self-reflect. Slipping happens to all of us, but if you can get yourself back on track quickly then you are winning.

Chapter 19: Finding Your Happy Place

Ever talked with someone that goes on about their 'happy place'?

You may be thinking, come on, what kind of hippie-dippie concept is a happy place (other than some pop-up exhibit that travels from city to city bringing colors and unicorns to eager customers in search of photo ops and childlike feelings)? But rest assured, it's brilliant and it's lifesaving. That's what a happy place can do for you.

Making the cognitive decision to go to a happy place is not only a choice you make, but it's also a boundary you set in your life. You've made the conscientious decision to be in a place with euphoric feelings and emotions. You may go there to get temporarily away from a situation, you may go there to avoid a situation, or you may go hangout there for a while just because you like that feel-good emotion. Whatever reason you go there, you've made your happiness, your well-being and your joy a priority.

In 1942, in the midst of World War II, young Ann Frank was gifted a red-checkered journal from her father. Like many Jews in Europe, the young Jewish girl and her family were forced into hiding to avoid being found by the Nazi's. Hitler, Germany's Dictator, and head of the Nazi's, had rallied his army and sent his troops forward with one mission: world domination with one pure race.

At the time, the Germans were making their way across Europe, and the world had officially become embroiled in a second world war. When young Ann Frank had been gifted her precious journal the war had already been ongoing for a treacherous 3 years, with no real end in sight. The Nazi's seemed to have the upper hand. Jews and other non-Aryan races were forced to live in ghettos, that is until they could be picked up and transferred to one of many concentration camps, also referred to as death camps. Thirty million Jews were sent to these camps over the course of the war, and 6 million never made it out alive. An additional 5 million non-Aryan race humans were massacred alongside them (13). Though the total number of deaths are unknown, over the span of World War II, 70-85 million deaths globally were reported (14).

Whereas most teenagers are experimenting with life, learning how to drive a car, starting to test the world with their own freedoms, starting to eyeball the opposite sex, Ann Frank's teenage years were quite the opposite. Ann was locked away with her family, hiding from the world. Every unfamiliar noise, every knock at the door, every voice in the street was a prompt to stay silent, not even a breath should be heard lest they be discovered and carried away.

But amidst the chaos, in the depths of the most egregious acts of terror and war, even young Ann Frank found her happy place: with a pen and a red checkered journal.

She wrote in her first entry to her friend Kitty stating "I hope I will be able to confide everything to you, as I have never been able to confide in anyone, and I hope you will be a great source of comfort and support" (15).

That pen was the catalyst to take what was in her head and move it to paper. Her journal housed her thoughts, her dreams, her deepest secrets. In the midst of the war, Ann found what so many of us cannot find when there is panic and pandemonium: a happy place.

Writing is a sense of freedom, you can put anything on paper. It can be fiction or nonfiction, we can make a story, or we can pull from a factual source. When my best friend committed suicide, like many of those impacted by suicide, I didn't have any closure to the situation. I remember getting the call from my mother as I was living in Italy and I sat there motionless as I tried to comprehend what she was saying. I was left with questions, a broken heart, and a void in my life. So, I picked up a pen and I started writing. I wrote an entire story about a woman that got a call that her best friend had attempted suicide, and she ran from her life in Italy to go sit by his side. She got to hold his hand, she got to brush his blonde hair out of his sad blue eyes, she got to be there as he left the world. He didn't live, but she had the closure she needed, and peace restored in her mind. While that wasn't how my reality had unfolded, just putting my thoughts and wishes on paper brought me some small sense of closure and peace.

My happy place, much like Ann Frank's, was found with nothing more than a pen and paper. The solace in the turmoil, the comfort in the pandemonium, the peace in the chaos, the freedom in the storm.

It's entirely possible to have the world moving around you at a thousand miles a minute and to be completely at peace, in a happy place, but it's your decision to be there or not.

Ann could have chosen to panic and run out in the streets when she heard a noise coming, but instead, she grabbed her pen. She had two choices: to live in fear, to panic, to breakdown, or to do what was in her control which was to take a deep breath and write.

A happy place doesn't have to look like colors and unicorns, it is just a place where you find enjoyment, where you find freedom, where you feel happy.

It could take the form of something you do or something you think about.

For many, a happy place is found in meditating and creating visuals in their mind. It could be as exotic as sitting on a luxury hut on an island in Fiji, or it could be a memory of your child when they were first born, or maybe it's both.

The beauty of the mind and in creating your space that brings you joy is you decide what life looks like. You create where you go to. You create your response. There's no right and there's no wrong with how they should look.

Why do we need a happy place?

Gives a feeling of safety

That feeling of having a warm meal on a cold day.

The nostalgia of eating your mom's homemade mac & cheese, topped with buttery toasted bread cubes after playing outside making forts all day.

The memory of when you won a blue ribbon for the hula hoop contest when you were six.

That feeling of making the winning 3-point shot on the basketball court.

Your toes in the white sand as you relax in your

Adirondack chair. Your Jackie-O sunglasses shielding the blinding rays from penetrating your eyes yet warming your skin as it resumes the glow you had the year before. Your drink sweats as you grab it, the cool drops run down your hand forming clusters of tiny sand balls under your armrest.

We feel safe with these thoughts, they put us in a good place. There's a comfort, there's a familiarity, there's a wave of positive emotion that pulsates through the body, there's a smile that comes alongside with the visual.

Have you been in a situation where you said, 'I just want to be home'? It's because, to you, home is safe, it's comforting, it's understood, it's familiar, it's that feel-good safe mac & cheese sensation to your soul.

Removes you from the situation

A happy place gives you somewhere to go to that keeps you feeling protected even in the midst of chaos. Maybe you find your joy in writing, in art, in meditation, in reading, in music, in cooking, or any of the million distractions you can find. Maybe it's merely closing your eyes and envisioning yourself in Fiji.

Let your imagination run wild and make sure wherever it goes that it takes you to some place happy. How does the water feel? Is it warm? What do you feel when you submerge yourself underwater? Are your eyes open underwater? What do you see? Are there fish? What color are they? How does the sand feel between your toes?

How much more at peace do you feel now that you envision yourself on that beach? Maybe you're more of a lake person, so imagine yourself there. Wherever it is and however you do it, going to your happy place will remove you from the situation.

Allows you to take a step back and look at the big picture

Ever tried to look at a Monet painting up close? Doesn't make a whole lot of sense, does it? Thousands of tiny brushstrokes brilliantly swirled together as a masterpiece. Up-close, all you can see are lines on a canvas, but from afar, you see the magnificent 'Starry Night' that was so beautifully crafted from Monet's mind, through his brush, to your eye.

When you are in the thick of the moment, it's often hard to make sense of what is happening. No one has the macro level vantage point, and no one has a magic 8-ball. Like every other human, all we can do is make the best sense of the information in front of us. To get there, sometimes we need to take a step back to try to take it all in.

When you consciously decide to go to your happy place, you are removing yourself from thousands of swirling lines on a canvas. You give your brain a break from the commotion and you can re-enter the situation with a newfound perspective.

Gives your patience a rest

Have you ever tried to put together something with a zillion little pieces, and as many times as you read through the instructions you just cannot put it together? You spend hours and hours fiddling with the tiny pieces, putting together and taking apart the contraption and still not succeeding. Ever taken a break and then started again when your patience wasn't completely shot? What happened? You did it, didn't you? All you needed to do was to take a step back and give your patience a rest.

Patience helps keep you level. Merriam Webster defines patience is "the capacity to accept or tolerate delay, trouble, or suffering without getting angry or upset." If you are worn out, tired, unable to process information, and flat out frustrated, then you are likely to become irritable, agitated, anxious, angry or upset.

Go to your happy place, give your patience a rest and come back renewed. You may find some level of clarity when you do go visit that happy place, or even figure out the missing step to building your zillion piece contraption called life.

Can make you aware of where you need to establish boundaries

In my book "RESET" I talked about a trigger word I used to put me into a happy place when I would start to get anxious. When I was in hot yoga one night I told myself that I could not leave until I had a word to think of every time I started to get anxious. I laid there at the end of my hour of stretching and meditating and for several minutes. I thought of what would bring me instantaneous joy. What one word could I say that would give me immediate happy thoughts? My best friend had recently told me she was pregnant and there it was. That unborn gem of a human was going to be the name I said every time I felt myself getting angry, anxious, or in a panic.

For the next few weeks, I monitored how many times I was saying this little boy's name and I was shocked. I realized that I allowed myself to get worked up far too often and that I needed to establish boundaries in my life to protect me from living in this emotional state.

I used my happy place (my trigger word) to not just calm myself down, but it ultimately helped me to assess my life and where putting boundaries would prove useful.

Redirects your mind and gives it another option

Having a happy place gives your brain another path to
walk down. When you're standing in front of that
Monet. when you're fiddling with that widget, when
you're glued to the television where they keep talking
about the stock market dropping, when people are
dying from an unrecognizable virus and you can't seem
to avoid the question in your mind about how you're
going to make it through, then redirect your mind.
Give your mind another option and take it to a happy
place
Whatever your happy place looks like, think through it
now and pull on it when you start to feel anxious,
panicked, stressed, overwhelmed, or any other feeling
that raises your blood pressure. It could be that one
trigger word puts you in a happy space. Maybe it's the
scenario you craft in your mind where you tap into all
of your senses and imagine yourself in another place.
Or perhaps you engage in a physical activity that
brings you joy. There's no limit to how many happy
places you can have or how you get there, but they're
useful.

A happy place is a boundary, and you have to protect it
as such. It's a place you make the decision to go when
you are feeling anxious, or it might just be a place
where you enjoy spending your time. Whatever reason
brings you there, treat it as sacred. If your happy place

is the gym, do not read the news or do work while you're exercising, focus on the sweat, the gains, the pump. If your happy place is reading a book, do it with the TV turned off. If your happy place is a bubble bath, lock the door behind you and keep out all distractions. If there is something that could taint the space where you find enjoyment, then make sure you keep them separate (that's a boundary). If you taint your happy place with negativity, anything that would ruin the moment, then you jeopardize the enjoyment, the peace, the pleasure you get when you go there. Keep it sacred.

Chapter 20: Breaking out of panic mode

It's far too easy to get caught up in the pandemonium. Even when you have boundaries in place, if you're caught in the thick of it all then it's easy to get swept away. Ever seen a tornado? It will barrel through a town unapologetically and pick up anything in its path. Bits and pieces of homes and buildings and entire vehicles get eaten and thrown around by the swirling winds. And like whirling dervishes, the tornado spins across its dance floor until the performance is over. And when it is, debris is strewn in every direction. Lives are shattered.

Hard not to get picked up and head in the direction of the wind, it's strong and everyone else is going in the same direction.

As our plane made its way into the Charlotte airport I felt a pain under my ribs. My ex-husband and I were on our way to my sister's graduation, not a good time to feel ill. The wheels hit the pavement and my body winced in pain.

'What is going on' I thought.

My ex grabbed my backpack and we made our way down the narrow steps of the little puddle hopper airplane and slowly made our way indoors. No sooner had we started to feel the cool AC touching our skin than my mind started to race. I felt the push on my ribcage intensify and my breath was progressively getting shorter and shorter. Was this the gallstone the Italian doctor told me I had 5 years before? Was I about to have a ruptured gallbladder? Was I going to explode from the inside out?

"Jen, why don't you sit down."

I sat down in the middle of the airport and found myself barely able to breathe. My ex had called over the paramedic and before I knew it I was laying down on the ground with a ventilator over my face. It was surreal and it happened fast. One minute I was headed to my sister's graduation, and the next I was headed to the hospital.

The paramedics put me on a stretcher and loaded me into the ambulance.

This was a first for me.

They rolled me into the emergency room and started doing tests.

My parents had been driving the trek from Virginia to watch their youngest daughter graduate from South Carolina University and were coincidentally not far from Charlotte when this all happened. My ex called and routed them over to the hospital.

I didn't even know what was all happening to me, but not too long after I got to the hospital I was finally able to breathe. My inability to take in a deep breath had been restored and I was now able to carry on a conversation. My anxiety and panic had leveled, I no longer thought my insides were going to burst out of my body.

My parents arrived, and they, along with my ex, stood in the room with me as the doctor gave me the news.

"Ma'am", the doctor said as he stood alongside my bed," it looks like you had case of gas."

"You've got to be joking me?"

I looked around at the people I loved the most, rallying to show their love and support on my, what I thought, near death experience, turns out I just had a case of the gas. Oh-my-WORD!

"Ma'am, you went into a panic attack, but the good news is you're fine. I'd suggest that next time you start to get a shortness of breath that you sit down, put your head between your knees and count to 100. You can be released."

Well, that was an exciting and expensive adventure that a $5 box of Gas-X probably could have handled.

What happened? How did I get so worked up?

When a tornado of bad news and the negative thoughts

start swarming, they tend to go faster and faster, picking up speed and intensifying. Before you know it, you're in full on panic mode. Had I just sat down and put my head between my knees then I could have probably avoided the whole situation and been down in South Carolina celebrating with my sister.

The best way to stop yourself from going down a path of panic and paranoia is to stop it before you get there. Once you get sucked up into the tornado or full on into your panic attack then it may get worse before it gets better, but you can still work yourself out of it.

Look, I understand that sometimes there is no avoiding the news. Social media, television, texting, group chats, conversations with friends and family- it's inevitable that news is going to cross your path at some point during the day. It seems the majority of the news is dark and depressing, only small bits and pieces are left for the 'feel good' and 'good Samaritan' stories. It's good to be informed, it's good to keep up to date with what laws are changing and how the government is responding. But, there's a difference between watching the news and taking in the facts vs. creating hysteria in your mind that launches you into that state of panic.

Maybe the doctor was right. Maybe you need to sit down, put your head between your legs and count to 100. It's actually not a bad idea, certainly one approach.

What the doctor was suggesting was that I remove

myself from the situation and do breathing techniques that have proven to be calming. You have every right to turn off the TV and go meditate, or go to your happy place, or change the conversation entirely. You are not committed to staying glued to the television or to even entertain the conversation you're having.

If you have set a standard in your life that you want to be happy, then your boundary response is to keep anything that is not happy in nature at bay. Again, staying informed and panicking are different. You choose how you are going to take in the information. That funnel, that filtering, all happens in your mind, use your mind boundaries.

Stay connected to your thoughts, your feelings, and what is happening around you. Don't just allow anything to stick in your mind, be strategic.

Why do music companies put a warning label on some of their music? Because not all people want to listen to music with explicit lyrics. Consumers often make the decision upfront whether to purchase the album or not based on the content of the lyrics. Same with movies. Many parents will not allow young children to watch R-rated movies because they are too graphic and disturbing to process at such a young and impressionable age.

Understanding what you are consuming is a responsibility that you own. If you choose to listen to hate music, it will likely have an influence on your perception, your mood or how you think. Funnel the right messages into your brain and know the difference.

'Jen- when I hear the news that the country is under attack, how do I not go into panic mode?'

Valid question. What I would tell my clients is this, 'what do you control in the situation?' You don't control the attackers, you do not control the where. You do, however, have the control over your response. If you choose to panic, then that is your choice. If, however, you choose to look at the situation opportunistically, look for lessons, look for the silver lining, look for the good in it all, stay inside and follow the instructions from leadership officials, then that too is a choice you can make.

I would ask, 'where is your power in all of this?' What so many of us forget is that we own our power and need to take responsibility for ourselves. That is, until or unless we give it away.

> *When we play the victim, when we make excuses, when we hit the panic button, then we give up our power. If we forget we have choices, then we give up our power. If we allow our boundaries to be crossed, then we give up our power.*

So, I'll ask again, 'where is your power in all this?'

I think sometimes we just need a reminder that we have choices. Once we get that, then you need to focus on what you control, it's as simple as that.

First, you need to be aware that it's happening. You need to recognize where you are at and make the decision that it is not where you want to be. Then, step away, find a quiet spot, go to your happy place, or do a darn good job of filtering the information and using those mental boundaries to keep the negativity in the gutter and your mind in the middle of the lane. That's how you break out of panic mode.

Stick your head between your knees, breathe and regroup. Find your power. Armor your mind.

~~~~

To complete the story of the trip to the hospital for my near death-by-gas experience, when I finally made it down to South Carolina there was a woman that approached me at my sister's graduation party.

"Weren't you the one who was taken out on a stretcher in the Charlotte airport? We felt so bad for that poor girl. I'm so glad you're ok."

My little escapade didn't just impact me. It impacted my parents, my ex, the hospital staff, the paramedics that got me to the hospital, and even the random passerby who got to witness what looked like could be a tragedy in the making.

The way you respond to life has a direct impact not just on your own life and your well-being, but on other people as well, even if you think you're hiding something. Panic mode can be contagious, so best to avoid it all together. Understand your power, which you still have in panic mode, you just need to take it back because you've given it up at that point.

Chapter 21: When do we give up our boundaries?

By now you know that boundaries are power. They are your personal limits. You define them, you own them, you manage them. And although they are power, sometimes we give them up without even realizing it.

Ever tried to give a teenager a curfew? Thinking back to when you were a kid and also asking around to some of the other parents you thought for your 15-year-old kid that 11pm was more than fair. In fact, when you were that age it was 10:30pm max, or you'd get grounded. 11pm seemed fair and generous.

For the first 3 months everything seemed fine, by 11:01pm you'd hear the door open, shut, then lock. But shortly thereafter you started to notice your teenager is coming in by 11:09pm, then 11:16pm, then 11:21pm. You didn't say anything because it's relatively close to 11pm. Before you knew it, your teenager started coming home past midnight. Mind you, this is your teenager who isn't even able to drive yet.

What happened?

You established your rules and guidelines, you said be home by 11pm. How does your teenager think that coming home after midnight is acceptable? How did this line get crossed so far?

Simple.

You allowed it.

It's great to establish boundaries, but if they are not communicated, if they are not enforced, if they vary, then you've established a suggestion, not a boundary.

When do you give up your boundary?

When you are unclear

When you are unclear in what you are wanting, then you leave it up to the other person to interpret what you are saying.

Imagine you ask your partner to bring home dinner. She stops by the store and gets you fried chicken with mashed potatoes, cornbread and huge slice of cake. She knows it's your favorite, and since she loves to make you smile she thought this would be a great idea.

Knowing that you were going to be working in your home office until late, she not only brought home your meal but she took the time to put it on a plate with real silverware and brought it to you. She places the meal in front of you and she sees you scratch your head as you stare at the plate.

"Everything ok?"

"It's great, no really, thank you. I just wanted to eat

healthy. I told myself I needed to lose weight and I was really hoping you'd bring home a salad."

Sound familiar? Has this ever happened to you?

The truth is, you really can't fault her because you never told her you wanted to lose weight. She was acting out of kindness and love, so you know that next time you need to be more clear.

Now, imagine you told your spouse that you need to lose weight and she still brought you the meal with the huge piece of cake. You might still scratch your head, because cake is really not a diet food, but she still had good intentions and maybe she might not have known any better.

Let's try it again. Imagine you told your spouse that not only do you need to lose weight, but that you want a healthy salad with chicken and a side of watermelon. Now, if she comes home with fried chicken, mashed potatoes, cornbread and a huge slice of cake - then yes, I would scratch my head too, because you were clear in what you wanted.

Making sure you are clear in your communication, what you are asking for, the rules you set for yourself will minimize, if not eliminate, ambiguity. Additionally, you can make sure your needs are met so you are satisfied. Don't give up your boundaries by being unclear.

When you do not stand firm on your boundaries

If you do not stand behind your boundary then it no longer is a boundary. Back to the teenager and his curfew. The parents started off with the right intention, they established a curfew rather than letting the teenage decide. But, this quickly diminished when the parents didn't enforce it.

Imagine if the teenager had a consequence associated with coming in after 11:01pm. What if the XBOX or their phone was taken away, or they were grounded, or they didn't get their allowance? The teenager may come in after 11pm, but I guarantee they are going to weigh the importance of their XBOX or phone privileges against that extra hour.

Stand firm on your boundaries and enforce them, then you won't give them up.

Allow abusive behaviors in your life

Abuse is never acceptable behavior. Read that again. Abuse is NEVER acceptable behavior. And abuse is not just physical. It's manipulation, it's greed, it's mental, it can come in so many forms, and never are acceptable behaviors.

If you allow abuse into your space then you have broken a boundary because abuse should never be tolerated.

When you say YES when you really mean NO

Ever said YES when you really meant NO? Don't lie to yourself, think about it. Has someone ever approached you and you were prepared to say NO, but then you looked into their big blue eyes and couldn't help but say YES?

You've been saving your money for years to buy yourself the purse of your dreams. You're entirely different than your best friend, you take good care and pride in your belongings. You aren't reckless like some of your friends with their money, you're meticulous and you save and price shop for just the right thing. When you get a purse you've worked for it, you've saved for it, it wasn't just last week's paycheck.

Louis Vuitton. The name just sounds expensive, and it was. You told yourself you weren't going to let anyone borrow it, especially your best friend because God only knows how many purses she's ruined by spilling bottles of perfume, pens bursting, or food leaking all over the interior. This was your purse to be enjoyed selectively.

You knew she was going to ask, she wished she had a Louis, but she's also not very good with her money. You prepare yourself in your mind that you are going to say NO. Your boundary is NO. Your rule is no borrowing of the purse.

As you prepare to go out one Friday night, she comes over and gets ready at your place. She's going through your closet while you're in the shower and happens upon the purse.

"Hey! Is this your new purse you got?"

In your mind you immediately tell yourself that she needs to put it down, step away, and not allow her clumsy self near your prized possession.

You get out of the shower, grab your robe, and make your way over to your closet. And there she is, dressed with an outfit that matches your new purse perfectly. She's dancing around and smiling, she loves it.

"Can I borrow it?"

You want to say NO, but you cave.

The next morning, you see your new white Louis with a stain not only on the inside, but also the outside. You're infuriated. But, with whom? Your friend, or with you?

If you have a boundary, keep it. If you want to say no but you say yes, then it's not a boundary.

It's not enough to establish boundaries and communicate them, you also need to uphold them. If you are unclear, if you flat out don't uphold them, if you allow abusive behaviors in your sphere or if you say YES when you really mean NO then you are not staying true to yourself. You take the power away that you established for yourself and you essentially threw them aside.

Uphold the boundaries you establish, it's the only way people will respect them, and ultimately respect you. Don't allow your boundaries to become suggestions when they should or should not be enforced. Not only is it confusing to you, but to everyone else in your life.

Imagine if you changed your mind every other day on what boundaries you wanted to uphold. Sometimes you would allow your friend to borrow your purse, other times you would not. Your friend would certainly not know what to expect and might even think you were a little bi-polar. Your boundaries shouldn't be confusing, they should be consistent.

Ever thought of someone as a pushover? Someone that allows people to walk all over them that even if they want to say NO they always say YES? Don't let that be you.

Don't let your boundaries be suggestions. If you treat them as a suggestion, then they get upheld as suggestions. This is not only poor communication, but you will not get the respect from yourself (your self-esteem will be impacted) or from those in your life. You'll lead people down a confusing road where both they and you will be uncertain how and when to act a certain way. You'll find yourself fighting this uphill battle of trying to have balance in your life, but you'll keep having to reestablish it if you aren't consistent.

Establish your boundaries and hold yourself and others to them, otherwise you're giving them up.

Chapter 22: Keys to Success

Life has a lot of moving pieces. If I start to think about all the *should-do's* and then couple that with trying to do everything right, life can be a bit overwhelming.

- Eat right
- Cut back on sugar
- Don't eat foods high in cholesterol
- Exercise
- Get enough sleep
- Volunteer
- Be a good leader
- Provide for the family
- Be active in your kid's life
- Socialize with friends
- Go to church
- Pay bills on-time
- Pray
- Call your parents
- Keep your vehicle clean
- Do something nice for yourself
- Self-reflect
- Read
- Do laundry
- Change your sheets
- Put the dishes away
- Go to the doctor

- Go to the dentist
- Go to the optometrist
- Donate money to good causes
- Take care of the pet's daily needs
- Make sure food is on the table
- Take your pet to the vet once a year

The list goes on and on and on. How do you make sure that you are maintaining your balance when you have so much to keep track of? How do you know when you're off balance and how should you respond?

Back to the gut

Using your gut as your guide, if you are feeling like your life isn't balanced, then take a look at everything you have going on and how you are handling it. You may need to get quiet in your thoughts and ask your higher power to reveal what is off-track or out of balance. If you are feeling something isn't right, then it probably is not. Maybe it's more boundaries you need, maybe you simply need to take on less, but if your gut says something is off, then it's time to pay attention.

Self-reflect

As you get into your quiet space, get back to those

feelings and ask yourself how you feel. You should be doing this every day, if not at all times during the day. If you can be honest with yourself then you will know when you are off-balance.

Make this a priority to do when you wake up or before you go to bed. What went well that day? What didn't go well? What could you have done better? What areas in your life do you not feel that sense of satisfaction?

The key here is to be honest and be consistent. Don't let life be that tornado and sweep you off your feet and toss you into your neighbor's yard before you realize it. Reflecting and getting intimate with yourself and your needs will keep you planted on solid ground.

Take care of you

During the COVID-19 crisis, I saw several people in my sphere nosedive. I'm talking about falling back into their addiction, falling into depression, or winding up in a psych ward. In each of these situations I asked the person what they had been doing for themselves recently amidst their hectic life- and not one of them told me they had done anything for themselves.

When you are not taking care of yourself then you are walking on a wire just waiting to fall. You can still be noble and take care of others while taking care of yourself because it's necessary.

When I was deep in my depression and not taking care of myself I was able to only do a fraction of what I'm able to do now. A small fraction. It's not a matter of 'if you'll fall' it's 'when you'll fall'. If you want to be that leader, if you want to be that person people look up to, if you want to be that caretaker, if you want to be happy and live your best life- then you need to make sure you are taking care of you.

Even superheroes need to sleep, so don't go after the world and try to go-go-go. You need to take care of yourself as well, so if you are not paying attention to your own needs then you will slip off-track, it's just a matter of time.

Taking care of you will help you find that balance.

Autopilot

Do you remember when you started driving? Your instructor took you on open roads, no more than 2 lanes, and you stopped at a stop light every half mile. You couldn't go fast even if you wanted to, there was no opportunity to go more than 40 miles per hour. When you learned how to park you were taken to an empty lot and you practiced going in and out of the spaces until you had demonstrated you were capable of parking.

Parallel parking was a whole different beast. Your instructor placed cones to serve the place of a pretend vehicle in front and behind the space you were aiming to park. It was a good thing they were only cones since you managed to run them over successfully on your first 8 attempts to park.

Once you were more comfortable and your instructor felt like you were ready to advance, you were taken out to a 4-lane road where you learned to merge with traffic. You were nervous and you felt your pits start to sweat as you cocked your head over your shoulder to catch any potential blind-spots in your vision so you could change lanes. You made the move and you sighed in relief because you managed to change lanes with cars zipping around you going 65 miles per hour.

It seems like that was only yesterday when you had to analyze every move and attentively watch every driver on the road. Now, it has become second nature to where you sometimes just go on autopilot.

Whenever you are learning something new, it will require more brain power and might even feel unnatural. This is perfectly normal! After some time and practice you will be on autopilot, just like your driving. It takes empty parking lots and driving over cones to get there, but that's all part of the learning.

You may feel unbalanced until you go on autopilot, but as long as you are not overdoing it (by listening to your gut and self-reflecting), and as long as you are taking care of yourself in the process, then it may feel a little imbalanced until you stabilize.

Scale up

When you're a new driver, it's not realistic to put yourself out on the main road right away, you need to ramp up and get comfortable. Going from relatively no boundaries to a plethora of boundaries overnight isn't best practice either. Not only might you need time to adjust, but also the people around you need to adjust to your new boundaries.

You'll know when it feels right because you're following your gut but be reasonable with yourself.

It takes time to learn and grow

Ever made the commitment to start going back to the gym and you decided that this summer you were going to have abs. No ifs, ands, or buts- you were getting abs. How long did it take before you started to see results? Did you make the commitment one day and see the fruits of your labor the next?

No.

Why?

It takes time to build muscle memory, it takes the right eating patterns, it takes time for your body to change. You'll have abs by summer if you stay at it, but it takes time to learn and grow.

Same is true with your boundaries. It takes time for you to settle in to the person you want to be. There are lots of amazing motivational speakers that have incredible stories, and it took them years to get to where they are today. Many of them had to scrape the bottom to reach the top. It was through those trials and challenges that they found the lessons that strengthened them to the person they evolved to.

When those influential people were going through their challenge or growth period, they didn't have all the wisdom they do today, they are teaching you now what they learned as a result of going through what they went through then. They're showing you what took time to learn, it wasn't an overnight journey.

If there was a magic wisdom pill then I'm sure many people would go buy it. Transformation takes time, so realize that it will not be instantaneous for you to come into your own.

Growth in challenges

Finding the growth and lessons in challenges is true

maturity. If you are constantly looking for learning opportunities, then you'll find how your perception completely transforms.

I think about this investment property I bought that I intended to build a house on. As soon as I leveled the decrepit home that was on the property when I purchased it, it got rezoned commercial. I ended up having to fight the county for 5 months, where I was finally given permission to build. I then ran into additional issues since I had a dry creek running through the property and had to prove it wasn't in the floodplain. Everywhere I turned there was an expensive issue that needed to be addressed. In the end, my life had taken some different twists and I decided I no longer wanted the property, but neither did anyone else.

I had sunk a lot of time and money into this property and it was going to keep eating away at my pocket until I could sell it. I finally had an investor that was seriously interested in the property, but the COVID-19 crisis hit at the same time and then he backed off.

I could have easily fallen into the victim mentality, or become enraged at the situation, but I have boundaries in place that tell me to not go there. Instead, I look for the lessons. What could I have done differently, or maybe what good did I do by having made the decision

I made?

There's a backstory with the property, I purchased this land and home from a woman whose family did a drug intervention to get her back on-track. The house was a hotspot for drug dealers and I had to force them to go elsewhere. I was told by all the neighbors that the neighborhood was now much quieter, and the dealers and users almost ceased to exist since I took over the property. I don't know why I ventured into this endeavor, but there were loads of lessons I learned along the way, and maybe the reason I was there was not just to learn, but to put good back in the world- I may never know.

What I do know is I now need to do a lot more upfront research with the county before I buy a property. This property had been for sale for two years, and there was a reason. Without consulting the advice of people much more educated on these types of investments, I proceeded forward on my own. That was a lesson learned. I also learned a lot by having taken down a house and all the many hoops the county made me jump through. And lastly, I know I put good back in the world and the children of that neighborhood could more comfortably go outside without the worry of drug deals happening.

Look for the lessons in challenges and grow them.

Surround yourself with people you want to emulate

Make sure you are surrounding yourself with people that are like you or that you want to emulate. Try to surround yourself with people that are further along in their careers, their life development, their business, their self-awareness. When you do, you can learn and grow from them.

Don't try to be the strongest one in your group, aim to be the one with the most to learn. It's easier to be raised up when you have a strong tribe around you, than to have to pick up an entire team yourself.

Remember, you are who you surround yourself by, so find people you want to be like and let them help be your guide.

Find a mentor/coach

Why do people get a trainer in the gym? The accountability, the encouragement, the push, the knowledge- it's having someone more well versed in a subject you want to master teach you and give you the knowledge they have studied for years.

Imagine you are 60 pounds overweight, but you think you are doing everything right. You try walking 3x a week, and you even have a body pump class you take once a week. It's not for lack of moving, and you've certainly stayed regimented over the years. You would even say you eat right since you've been doing a carb and gluten free diet for 3 years. You just keep seeing the scale get higher and higher and you can't figure out what you're doing wrong.

Time to consult an expert.

What might seem right to us may not in fact be right and it takes an expert to take a look and assess what is really happening. Not everyone's body responds to the same to food so it may be that you think gluten and carb free is what you need to be doing but in fact there's another solution. This expert may also tell you that you need to change up your workout routine; maybe add weights, running, or a couple of more classes a week. Maybe you need to be drinking less sugary drinks and increase your water, possibly it's as simple as that.

Guidance from someone that has a deeper knowledge in the field might be the exact thing you need to invest in to shed those 60 pounds. Same with your life. Life coaches and mentors are there to serve the same purpose as a trainer in the gym- to help you achieve your goals and to stay on track.

This mentor is someone you can confide in and bounce ideas off of. It should be someone whose qualifications you respect and probably someone you mesh with. You may not always like the advice, but it's the guidance you need. I don't always like my trainer at the gym when my muscles feel like they're going to fall off, but it's the push my body needs. Your coach or mentor should be the same, they may challenge you, but remember- you learn through challenges.

Life has so much it throws at you every day and in a world where we are all connected by technology, the number of 'things' we need to manage is potentially unlimited. It's easy to feel like we are off balance, and sometimes we legitimately are, or we might be growing. Feeling off-balance tells us something, and we need to be in tune and listen to our bodies.

Make sure you are taking care of you, that you are self-reflecting, scale up in your life (don't try to do it all at once) and look for the lessons in the challenges. Surround yourself with like-minded individuals and even find a coach/mentor to continue your growth, bounce ideas off of, and to learn from people that have walked in your shoes.

Don't be afraid to talk to people, tap into your resources, and most of all- don't be dishonest or neglect yourself. Life is a balance, and once you get it, you start to go on autopilot, but that takes time. Be realistic with yourself and set realistic goals and expectations.

Chapter 23: It's in you

The only thing in between you and your happiness is you.

That's a powerful statement, so digest it. You have all of the tools inside of you, it's awakening them and using them is what you need to master, but what you have is already in you.

Two-time Emmy award winner, Kristen Joosten, raised her family while working as a nurse. Kristen knew there was more inside of her, and when she was 56 years old she packed up and moved in with her son in Los Angeles. Whereas many may have thought this was a closed chapter for her, Kristen proved them wrong and found herself on the set of Desperate Housewives and won not just one, but two Emmys for her acting.

Kristen had it in her, she always did. She had the ability to be that actress she knew she could be her whole life and she finally stepped out and into her innate ability.

Your power is in you, it's just awakening it in you and stepping into the life you were meant to have. There is no one that will take responsibility for your life other than you, so if you want happiness, all it takes is some self-reflection, actions, communication and practice.

Making the connection

I think of how many times I thought of something and couldn't bring my thoughts out and voice them. Or how many times I thought of something and I couldn't get my thoughts and my actions to connect with each other.

How often are you in your head and you have one dialogue, but what you say and what you do don't match? It's frustrating. You are thinking something and the words or the actions don't follow. Where is the disconnect?

When I moved to Italy I didn't speak a lick of Italian. Learning another language is an interesting process, and it took a lot of time and dedication on my part. I listened to language tapes, read language books, I had a dictionary in my pocket that I constantly referenced (this was before the age of smartphones).

When I made the commitment to learn Italian I did everything I could to saturate my head with learning. Italian movies with English subtitles, English movies with Italian subtitles, listening to Italian songs, I even watched Soap Operas (think of the level of dialogue-about as basic as basic could be), and I am not the type to watch these kinds of shows- or any TV for that matter. I wanted my brain to be flooded with this romantic language so I could communicate with my roommates and the wider Italian population (not to mention, I wanted to communicate with my boyfriend's parents- that would have been a huge win!).

We aren't aware of learning a language when we are children, but as an adult it was an interesting process as I observed myself learning to speak. I started to understand words faster than I could find my tongue. I remember sitting at the table with my boyfriend and roommates and they were having a conversation and for the first time I felt like I understood most of what was being said (many times I sat there and was lost until I was translated to). I was so excited when I realized I understood the conversation and I was ready to jump in.

I remember piping up and I could see that my friends saw I finally connected the dots in my head and was about to make a leap and be able to participate in the conversation. My head thought one thing, and my tongue in no way cooperated. I understood what was being said, but I couldn't form a response. My mouth opened and my tongue rolled out on the table with only a couple of words that made any amount of sense. It was frustrating. How could my comprehension be working but my audible message not reciprocate?

All I could do was laugh, but I really wanted to start talking with my friends!

A few days later after lunch I told my friend 'io devo

risposarmi'. My boyfriend looked at me, cocked his head and smiled. He smiled and said, I think you meant 'io devo riposarmi'. Unless you truly need to get remarried instead of resting. Instead of communicating 'I must rest' ,I told everyone randomly 'I must remarry.' One simple letter changed the context of my sentence entirely. I finished my meal with a good chuckle.

Communication takes practice, and it may not always come out the way you intended it at first. If I gave up trying to learn the language then there were many situations and conversations I would have missed out on. I really did try to do the best I could, I studied cultural norms, I was inundated with movies and television, I read and highlighted that dictionary I always kept it in my pocket for goodness sake. I did the best I could, and when my tongue and brain didn't connect I just kept trying. It was finding my voice and was willing to take advice from others when the message wasn't clear enough.

I knew I goofed when I said I wanted to remarry, I could see it on everyone's face. I didn't mean to say that, but seeing the expressions on their faces made me aware of my mistake. Pay attention to the way others react and respond when you communicate. Are you getting the response you desired? Did you feel good about your delivery? Do you think your internal dialogue was well represented in the conversation?

Did you hold back on anything you wanted to say because you weren't comfortable, you were afraid of the backlash, you didn't want to upset anyone or cause any confrontation? What does your internal gut say about the situation? Keep tweaking until you are getting the results you want and don't hold back.

You are not always going to 'get your way' and the intended outcome may be different than you envisioned. If you are being honest with yourself and you know you can communicate your boundaries and your piece in their entirety and in the best possible way, then you have a free conscience and an improved self-esteem. If you haven't, then you need to keep practicing.

At the end of the day you are the one that gets to deal with any internal guilt or emotions about your situation. Your gut and conscience will let you know if you are not being true to you, if you are being honest with yourself. Any dissention should be a red flag that you have work to do.

Give yourself some grace. Effective communication and even knowing how to handle a situation might not come on the first time. If you give up though, it will never come. Just keep at it and you'll be resting (and not remarrying) after lunch before you know it.

Shift gears when life throws you a curveball

Wouldn't it be nice if life always went the way we intended it to?

Maybe.

I don't believe that life is always going to work out the way I think it will, and I've come to accept that my higher power has a much larger perspective of the situation and will guide me in a different direction and keep me on the right path. I know that I only have a microcosmic view of my world, and I believe that there may be something better out there for me yet I don't always know it at the time.

Remember the song "Unanswered Prayers" by Garth Brooks? I'm dating myself, but in his hit song he talks about wanting to marry this certain woman and he prayed and prayed over it. Turns out, life threw him a curveball and they didn't end up together. Instead, he found another woman, and this woman ended up being the love of his life. In the song, Garth thanks God for his unanswered prayer, because if he had married the first woman- then he wouldn't have met the second.

If you arm your mind that curveballs will happen then when they do you will be prepared for them. You will recognize that you were on the wrong track, or there's a lesson to learn. You may not know the reasoning for the change, but you will know it was meant to happen.

It's a tiny shift in how you think. It's looking at that glass half empty and shifting to saying it's half full. Something moves you off the course you 'think' you're on and now instead of being a victim, you claim victory. From victim to victorious in just a small shift in your mind. It's your perception, and your perception is your reality.

As Sumner Redstone said "Success is not built on success. It's built on failure. It's built on frustration. Sometimes it's built on catastrophe." Do you let one 'failure', one 'frustration', one 'catastrophe' take your joy, or do you see it as a building block to your success? You choose- it's in you.

Know Your Rights

Remember, you have basic inherent rights and you should not be afraid to use them. You can be treated with respect, you can say no, you can put yourself first, you are allowed to feel the way you want. You own these rights, they are in you and only you can give them away.

If someone does not respect these rights or your boundaries then you have the right to walk away. If there is not mutual respect between two people, then is it a reasonable relationship that should be kept alive? The respect could be in regards to time or investment. It does not always have to be if you have respect for the person.

I think back to a 'friend' who thought she had the right to call me only when it was convenient for her. When I tried calling or needed something, she was rarely there. Ever felt like you were driving the wrong way on a one-way street. That's how this friendship felt, it was inequitable and I ultimately walked away. I knew it was my right to be respected, and I didn't get that feeling from her. No harm no foul- I just walked away. The funny thing was, it didn't seem to be a big deal to her, so why was I investing my time into someone who really didn't value me back. I wish her well, but she will not steal my joy, I will not be disrespected, and this will not be a one-way street- I have the right to make that decision.

If the law does not hold people responsible for the laws that govern the land, then are they really laws- or are they just suggestions? You do not want to govern your life with a list of suggestions, it's an invitation to have what you truly deem important to be overlooked and those lines crossed.

I'm going to say this and I know it's going to come off strong. You take ownership in how you allow people to treat you. If you continue to allow someone to treat you poorly then that is on you. Have your boundaries, know your rights and be treated the way you know you deserve to be treated. You are the CEO, you are the big boss, you are the one and only one that is standing between you and your happiness.

If you can wrap your mind around the fact that there is something better for you out there then you still win when life changes directions.

If you learn to communicate not just to others, but also to yourself then watch your self-esteem rise.

If you decide to learn through the challenges instead of playing a victim, then you are winning when life changes directions.

If you know your rights and exercise them then you govern the law over your domain.

If you believe there is something bigger and better for you in store when something doesn't go your way, then life will always be in your favor.

If you can put up your mental and emotional boundaries and tell yourself that you are not going to be swept away when panic and fear could creep in, then you are armed by boundaries.

If you tune your perception to positivity and optimism then watch your perception become your reality. Life is a mind game and it's all in how you view your world. No one can tell you otherwise. If you want to be Superman when you grow up, then you believe you will be Superman. If you tell yourself that you amount to nothing then you won't, even if the rest of the world disagrees with you. It doesn't matter what the world thinks, it all comes down to you. Tune yourself to the channel you want to listen to and become that Superman character. It's all in you and it's just tuning in and dialing up what is innately in you.

The Tibetan Lama, Sogyal Rinpoche once said, "You cannot ask the darkness to leave. You have to turn on the light." Flick that switch to 'ON'. Take charge and own your you again.

Chapter 24: What's the price you pay?

You always have choices, and the reality is you don't need to change anything in your life if you don't want to. If you want to stay right where you're at and live with panic, anxiety, low self-esteem, people walking all over you, you can, it's a choice.

You may decide that all this is just too much for you to want to set up in your life, and you'd rather take the time and pick up a hobby or spend more time reading. This is certainly a choice you have, but at what cost?

What is the cost to you not addressing your happiness?

You impact others

Just like others can influence your life, you also have an influence in the lives of people around you. You might have a spouse or partner, you might have kids, you might have coworkers, you might have family and friends, and guess what- you have an impact on each one of those people!

If you are down and dreary then you are not likely to be causing a positive impact. What an awful thought to think that you are negatively impacting people's lives because you didn't self-reflect and put the right boundaries in place in your life to bring yourself happiness. Instead, like a rock, you dragged your family and friends down whenever you were around and you pumped them full of negative thoughts and energy. That's a tough pill to swallow.

Take responsibility for your life and for your actions, and make sure that you are impacting the lives of people in your personal space for the better.

You have only one life

What I would hate for you is to live a life of regret. A life where you get to the end of it and you wish you had done things differently. There is only one thing in this life that is guaranteed and that is death. Everyone is guaranteed to die, but not everyone lives. I want you to live the life you have been given and get to that end point and look back fondly.

Sure, we are all going to think of things we probably could have done a little differently, but I want you to look back and be satisfied with your life. Did you live it happily or were you just existing?

I moved to California from Virginia to this small town halfway between San Francisco and Sacramento. For the entire six months there I found myself just existing to get through the experience. I didn't do anything to try to make it enjoyable. When I look back at that experience, it was the loneliest time in my life, I was literally just existing with little to no joy in my life. Fortunately, this was a short stint in my life, but some people go through their entire lives and they are just existing! Don't make this you!

You have one life, live it! It might not be perfect, but what is? Don't exist, look back and feel proud that you lived a life with fond memories and you can proudly say that you did the best you could with what you had. When I lived in California for that brief time, I didn't give it a chance, and I do not look fondly at the experience or how I handled it. One life, that's it. Live it.

Do you want to make a difference?

When you look at what you want to do with your life, do you want to make a difference? Maybe this is in the life of one or maybe in the lives of many. If you are living a life where you are constantly being taken advantage of, if you allow people to walk all over you, if you are constantly fighting a fight that you just never seem to win, then are you being effective in the areas where you want to make a difference?

I was constantly frustrated because I knew I had so much potential and yet I dealt with an addiction that held me back from meeting my potential. Once I had the right boundaries and my mindset turned around, then I was finally able to start making a difference in the lives of others and giving back in the way that I always wanted, but never could.

What's the legacy you want to leave?

How do you want to be remembered in your life, while you're here and when you're gone? Do you want people to remember you as the 'Scrooge' or the 'Miserable Human' or 'That Guy'? NO! You want to be known as someone that people speak fondly about.

You don't have to aspire to be Martin Luther King or Mother Theresa. You don't have to do anything profound that makes it into the history books to leave a legacy. You might leave a legacy by raising your children right, or bringing joy to people's lives, or even writing a book. You don't have to change the world to be a legacy maker, so don't get discouraged if you think that's what a legacy means. You define this, how do you want to be remembered, what impact did you have on the world (even if that's just your immediate world).

There's a price you pay for neglecting to wake-up and be the best you every day. It's your happiness, it's your joy, it's your self-esteem, it's your freedom, it's your time, it's your peace, it's the only life you've been given to live. What is it worth to you to not take the time and do the work? I'll tell you, it's more costly not to than it is to get it on track. Don't be at the end of your life and wish you had done it differently. You never know when your end day will come, so don't let life slip by while you keep promising yourself that tomorrow will be the day you start.

Reality is perspective. You can create whatever world you choose, the power is all in your mind. You can choose how your world looks, it's only a minor shift in your mindset that will get you there.

You took that job as CEO because you knew you could turn the ship around. You *are* the CEO, now step into the role and become the boss that everyone looks up to and respects. Build your brand, become that person that others look up to and want to emulate. Most importantly, make that 5-year-old version of yourself proud because you grew into the person you knew you were capable of. Boundaries will get you there, and they will protect you from the world. If a pandemic sweeps through, if fear and anxiety sweep the globe then you are already armed for battle. Acknowledge it's a choice, focus on what you can control, set your standards, define your boundaries, find that happy place, learn to communicate, figure out what breaks you out of panic mode and go get the life you want with the respect you deserve!

You are that Venom F5. Engage what you have between those ears and shield yourself from what life throws at you and step into your power. Boundaries keep you in your game, so put up the bumpers, grab a ball, define that playbook and go get what you want in life!

About the Author

Jen Sugermeyer was inspired to create and write "Defining Your Boundaries" after she wrote the chapter on 'Standards and Boundaries' in her #1 Best Seller, "RESET". After having gone through her own transformation, Jen discovered the power of boundaries and the protection and power they give all of us in our daily lives. With the events of 2020, Jen felt compelled to write "Defining Your Boundaries" to help the world stay in a state of peace and power when the world was facing some tough economic hardships and peoples lives were turned upside down.

Professionally, Jen spent 15 years in corporate America; contractor to the Department of Defense and Department of State, and she worked in both the public and private sectors of corporations. She has lived and worked around the globe, including Washington D.C., Afghanistan, Virginia, California, Texas and even spent a couple of years in Italy. These days, Jen offers global services with her 1:1 coaching, motivational speaking and her books. She has been featured on CBS, NBC, FOX and a variety of magazines and multitude of podcasts around the globe.
Originally from Northern Virginia, Jen has settled in the great state of Texas where she spends her free time volunteering in the community, traveling the globe, doing photoshoots, boxing, running the lakes, doting over her gorgeous niece, Olive, and momma of a rescue kitty, Booger. You can find out more about Jen and her products and services on jensugermeyer.com.

Appendix:

1. Amadeo, Kimberly. The Balance. How Does the 2020 Stock Market Crash Compare With Others? Accessed April 6, 2020. https://www.thebalance.com/fundamentals-of-the-2020-market-crash-4799950

2. Merriam-Webster. Control. Accessed April 6, 2020. https://www.merriam-webster.com/dictionary/control

3. The Myers Briggs Foundation. The 16 MBTI Types. Accessed April 10, 2020. https://www.myersbriggs.org/my-mbti-personality-type/mbti-basics/the-16-mbti-types.htm?bhcp=1

4. Who Invented the Internet. December 13, 2013. History. Accessed April 10, 2020. https://www.history.com/news/who-invented-the-internet

5. What is the lowest temperature ever recorded on Mount Everest. Base Camp Excursion. Accessed April 11, 2020. https://basecamptreknepal.com/what-is-the-lowest-temperature-ever-recorded-on-mount-everest

6. Pallardy, Richard. Britannica. Chile Mine Rescue 2010. Accessed April 18, 2020. https://www.britannica.com/event/Chile-mine-rescue-of-2010

7. Chilean Miners: We never lost faith, we knew we would be rescued. Accessed April 18, 2020.

https://www.theguardian.com/world/2010/oct/13/chilean-miners-rescued-health

8. The 50 most influential Christians of all time. Accessed April 13, 2020. https://www.brainz.org/50-most-influential-christians-all-time/

9. Venom F5. Hennessy. Accessed April 18, 2020. http://hennesseyperformance.com/vehicles/hennessey/venom-f5/

10. Silvestro. Brian. 2020 Ferrari Roma Is a Sleek Twin-Turbo V-8 Coupe With 612 HP. November 13, 2019. Accessed April 18, 2020. https://www.roadandtrack.com/new-cars/a29787948/2020-ferrari-roma-pictures-specs-hp-info/

11. 2020 Nissan Maxima. Accessed April 18, 2020. https://cars.usnews.com/cars-trucks/nissan/maxima/performance

12. Understanding your Miranda Rights. Accessed April 18, 2020. http://www.mirandawarning.org/whatareyourmirandarights.html

13. 11 Facts About the Holocaust. Accessed April 19, 2020. https://www.dosomething.org/us/facts/11-facts-about-holocaust

14. World War Two Casualties by Country. Accessed April 19, 2020. https://worldpopulationreview.com/countries/world-war-two-casualties-by-country/

15. Diary of Ann Frank. Accessed April 19, 2020. https://www.holocaustedu.org/education/research/this-week-in-history/june-12-1942-anne-frank/

www.ingramcontent.com/pod-product-compliance
Lightning Source LLC
LaVergne TN
LVHW091214080426
835509LV00009B/983